Narcissistic Abuse Recovery

Discover how to Recognize a
Narcissist and
Break Free from Emotional Abuse

Salena Douglas

Table of Contents

INTRODUCTION..7

CHAPTER 1: UNDERSTAND NARCISSISM...........10

WHAT IS NARCISSISM?...................................10
WHAT IS NARCISSISTIC ABUSE AND THE DIFFERENT TYPES...16

CHAPTER 2: NARCISSISTIC PERSONALITY DISORDER...22

TRAITS OF PEOPLE WITH NARCISSISTIC PERSONALITY DISORDER
....23
SIGNS OF NARCISSISM IN A RELATIONSHIP.......................29
SIGNS OF NARCISSISTIC PARENTING...............................34

CHAPTER 3: HABITS OF A NARCISSIST AND HOW THEY CONTROL PEOPLE...................................38

THE DIFFERENT TYPES OF NARCISSISTS...........38

HOW DOES A NARCISSIST CONTROL OTHERS?...................42

CHAPTER 4: HOW TO DEAL WITH A NARCISSIST. 48

HOW WOULD YOU RECOGNIZE A NARCISSIST?...48

KNOWING THAT YOU ARE IN A NARCISSISTIC RELATIONSHIP...50
DEALING WITH A NARCISSIST...............................53
IDENTIFY THE TYPE OF NARCISSIST YOU'RE DEALING WITH...53

CHAPTER 5: RECOGNIZE AND STOP A NARCISSISTIC ABUSE...59

UNDERSTANDING THE CYCLE OF ABUSE...........................59
HOW TO GET OVER NARCISSISTIC ABUSE QUICKLY.............66

CHAPTER 6: PROCESSING YOUR TRAUMA.........72

CHAPTER 7: STARTING YOUR RECOVERY JOURNEY
....78

STEPS TO LEAVING A NARCISSIST......................**78**

CHAPTER 8: START LOVING YOURSELF..............**94**

WHAT IS SELF-LOVE, AND WHY IS IT IMPORTANT TO LOVE YOURSELF? WHY SHOULD YOU CONSIDER BEING SELF-COMPASSIONATE AFTER?....................................94
STEP 1: EXERCISING FORGIVENESS...................98
ESTABLISH HEALTHY BOUNDARIES...................105
THE BASICS OF MEDIATION: WHAT EXACTLY IS MEDITATION? 111
BRIEF MEDITATION TECHNIQUES FOR A STRESS-FREE LIFE. .117
POSITIVE AFFIRMATIONS TO SAY EVERY DAY....................124

CONCLUSION...**125**

Introduction

Imagine you are in a relationship with the most perfect partner you could've ever dreamed of having in your life. The partner who checks all the boxes for being the most ideal person in the whole world. They are charming, attractive, and intelligent. But even after everything, you still feel like something is wrong.

The partner may seem loud, dominate the conversation, or even speak for the friend, even when the conversation is directed to them. The attention initially thought to be sweet seems more obsessive as the partner keeps track of every move the friend makes. The friend, who once had a boisterous and gregarious personality, now seems quiet, insecure, self-conscious, and guarded, hinting they may be mistreated in some way. But without any obvious signs of abuse, no one intervenes. This is what a narcissistic abusive relationship looks like from the outside and why narcissists can continue their behavior.

The worst part is that the victims in these relationships are either in deep denial that the problem is within the narcissist, or they've been made to believe all fault is theirs. Narcissistic relationships are often characterized by one person in control and the other person who is the victim. The victim usually stays in denial about their relationship with the narcissist because they fear being rejected or abandoned. They may also believe that they can change or fix the narcissist. However, staying in denial is a damaging strategy for both the victim and the narcissist.

Recovering from a narcissistic abuse relationship can be difficult because the abuser controls everything in the relationship. They often use psychological and emotional manipulation to keep their victim in line. Furthermore, victims of narcissistic abuse often have difficulty forming healthy relationships due to the past trauma they've experienced. Getting back on track can take a lot of patience, support, and recovery resources.

It doesn't care about gender, race, religion, social status, or other categories people are put into. Narcissists exist in every area of life, and so do their targets. Worst yet, victims believe they'll never do any better, keeping them in that invisible headlock without a fight. But it doesn't have to be that way.

Whether you are a victim or want to safeguard yourself for the future, this book is for you. Understanding the mindset of a narcissist, their personality traits, and their effects on those around them gives victims a new perspective of what they endured as well as a renewed sense of self. It's also a way to recognize the warning signs in future potential relationships so as not to repeat the cycle.

Throughout the book, we will go deep into what makes a narcissist tick, their MO, and how you can identify one. You will have a very good understanding of all the signs you should look out for, and in turn, how to defend yourself from all the different manipulative techniques. And if you are a recovering victim, don't worry, as we have covered you! There is an entire chapter dedicated to just helping recovering people understand how they can process their trauma and recover from their past abuse to lead a normal and healthy life.

It's hard to cut loose from a narcissistic relationship once they've got you wrapped around their little finger like a baby. If you've ever been the victim of a narc, or you're currently dealing with one, you'll find that no matter what happens or how bad things get, you keep returning to them. You know you'd be better off without them, yet, they have managed to get you so addicted to the trauma that it will take a lot of time before you can finally break free.

Dealing with the narcissist can have your mind and heart in a constant tug of war. In your mind, you know the narcissist is poison to your soul. But in your heart, you keep thinking about how much you love and need him, and you just can't let him go!

This tug of war keeps you in constant anxiety and self-doubt.

Next thing you know, you're used to being in this state, and you just can't let yourself see that there are other healthier states of mind to be in. So the narcissist damages you to the point that you're stuck on how great things were between you both in the beginning while at the same time denying the current reality of your situation. In other words, you're anything but present.

Sounds scary, right? The good news, though, is that with proper knowledge, it is possible to protect yourself and recover from an experience.

So, without any further delays, let's jump right in, shall we?

Chapter 1: Understand Narcissism

What Is Narcissism?

In its most basic definition, narcissism is an obsession with one's appearance and an overall sense of extreme vanity. Have you ever met someone constantly bragging about themselves and what they've accomplished, or who takes precedence over you in a conversation so they can brag about themselves more? For example, how about someone who seems to be constantly talking about themselves? Or perhaps someone who, no matter what happens, refuses to accept responsibility for anything? These individuals are referred to as "narcissists" for short. Narcissism is a personality trait almost everyone possesses; after all, narcissism is a relatively common personality trait. Being somewhat self-absorbed is an unavoidable aspect of the human condition. It is, in many ways, unavoidable in many situations. On the other hand, some people are so narcissistic that they can devastate their loved ones, causing pain that is difficult to quantify.

Although it's important to distinguish between "narcissism" and the medical condition known as "narcissistic personality disorder," it's also important to understand the difference between them. This book will be primarily concerned with the latter—it is simply the case that the coping mechanisms have remained largely unchanged. That is why we must establish a worst-case scenario, which you can modify —as you see fit —to ensure that it bodes well for your particular situation.

An individual with narcissistic personality disorder exhibits characteristics similar to those of the pure trait of narcissism; in fact, it is composed of characteristics considered narcissistic. Those who suffer from a narcissistic personality disorder, on the other hand, will exhibit significantly stronger manifestations of narcissistic traits, which are deemed significant in their ability to negatively impact their own lives as well as the relationships that they attempt to form in their lives.

Suppose you're talking about narcissistic personality disorder in the clinical sense. In that case, you'll hear it referred to either by the clinical term itself or by the term "narcissism." In light of the preceding, the question arises as to whether or not we can deduce any meaningful history of the term narcissism in the medical context.

Simply put, the modern definition of this term hasn't been around for very long, much like most things in medicine, especially mental health. According to medical conditions, it has had a short life span, which could be considered short.

The term "narcissism" has been around for quite some time in its general sense. It is generally understood as a reference to and an allegory for the myth of Narcissus from Greek mythology. As a young boy, Narcissus caught a glimpse of himself in the water and immediately fell in love with the face he was looking at. Finally, someone informed him that the reflection was only his own. As a result, he would never be able to truly love the object. As a result, he succumbed to his grief.

This idea of loving oneself so dramatically and intensely carves out the modern ideal of narcissism. It has been used to describe this specific kind of intense adoration of oneself for quite some time.

The term "narcissism" as used in medicine, on the other hand, has a more illustrious past. While its application as a general term is relatively straightforward, the story of its application as a medical term is more complicated and lengthy. We can begin by looking at the Freudian school of psychoanalytical thought as a starting point for this story.

According to Freud's school of psychoanalytical thought, most things in life are psychologically derived from the person's development at their core. However, there is a balance between conscious and unconscious thought at the end of the day. Of course, the psychologist Sigmund Freud was responsible for popularizing this school of thought. The Freudian's were a group of people who adhered to this particular school of thought.

What Causes Narcissism?

Narcissism is most often manifested in early childhood. People say narcissistic behavior reminds them of a toddler throwing a temper tantrum numerous times. Based on my own personal experience, I tend to agree with this statement. The emotional trauma that causes narcissism appears around the time of a toddler's development. As a result, the narcissist's ability to deal with emotions remains stuck at that stage of mental development. Isn't it true that this explains their potentially dangerous emotional immaturity?

We are all exposed to traumatic events during the early stages of our development. It's just a matter of time. As a child, trauma can be caused by something as simple as not being picked up by our parents when we are young or being forced to eat against our will. It could also result from something more serious, such as our mother abandoning us at kindergarten for the first time, resulting in a long-lasting fear of being separated from her. Our parents yelling and screaming at each other in our presence can leave imprints on our subconscious minds, as can our siblings. So, what kind of trauma results in the development of a narcissist? Having a parent who is either overbearing or completely neglectful of their children can cause their minds to be distorted, resulting in them becoming narcissistic adults later in life. Parents can be overprotective of their children's academic performance while being neglectful of their children's emotional well-being, as evidenced by their behavior toward their children in school.

The perceived lack of control is the source of trauma for a narcissist. Because they cannot acknowledge their own emotions, narcissists are extremely uncomfortable in their skin. They would feel that everything about themselves was wrong if they admitted one 'wrong' thing about themselves. As a result, every abusive and manipulative action they take solely makes them feel in command. You have absolutely nothing to do with the underlying cause of their toxic behavior toward you; it has everything to do with them. Keep your eyes peeled because they are projecting their own behavior, fears, and doubts onto you if you pay attention to what they say. A narcissist may lie frequently, but they will falsely accuse you of lying all the time— no matter how much evidence you provide to show that they are wrong. They may believe that everyone is out to get them and that they are always on the receiving end of the short end of the stick. As a result, they project their subconscious beliefs onto you by accusing you of plotting schemes against them every time there is a simple miscommunication. Always remember that narcissists were not taught how to express and process their emotions properly in the first place. While their parents may have been overly protective and proud of them, this was only true when they lived up to their parents' high standards. Perhaps some background research into the narcissistic personality of the individual in question could be undertaken? Even though it is frequently difficult to obtain a clear image. It is extremely difficult to discover the truth about a narcissist, especially when their parents admit they could not cope with their child's behavior. The majority of the time, one or both of their parents will exhibit some narcissistic characteristics themselves. It does not follow that the children of someone narcissistic are doomed to be narcissistic as well. At the end of the day, it is not your responsibility to figure out how the person who has treated you so badly came to be who they are today, nor is it necessary for your recovery process to do so. To recover from narcissists, you must first recognize that it is not your fault that they are one. You must also recognize that you are not responsible for the chronic toxicity that they have caused.

In some cases, this can result from the environment, resulting in a forced image of perfection later in life. Another factor to consider is abuse in early childhood. One strategy for coping with abuse is to consider yourself above it, or at least too clean for it. Narcissism is a protective barrier to keep the victim from being hurt again when an abusive past is considered. Even though there are numerous ways in which the disorder can be caused by the environment, there is some belief that the trait may, in fact, be hereditary. However, identifying a specific behavioral trait can be challenging in genetics. Even though it appears to be genetic, it is often the result of how the parents or grandparents were raised that causes the disease. This raises the question of genetics in its purest form.

On the other hand, science has not yet reached a definitive conclusion. Studies have not reached a conclusive conclusion. Because there are so many different conditions, it is difficult to determine which are caused by the environment and which are caused by genetics. Despite this, the vast majority of cases of narcissistic personality disorder can be traced back to the parents who raised the child. No matter the cause of the child's behavior - neglect, abuse, over protection, rewarding for insignificance, Munchausen's syndrome or even the parent instilling hypochondria or a sense of superiority in the child - the child's behavior is usually established at an early age. Because the disorder has such a deep-seated foundation and takes a long time to develop. It becomes even more difficult to overcome later in life. Changing someone's perspective on how they should see the world when they were raised and teaching them to see it differently can be nearly impossible. This can also result in an increase in behavioral and personality issues. Taking away the one, or the only, defense that someone has constructed to deal with trauma can leave them feeling exposed and vulnerable, leading to depression and/or anxiety. A narcissistic personality disorder progresses to high-risk avoidant personality disorder with agoraphobia and social anxiety, self-harm and suicidal ideation, and the intent to harm others. Treating people who use narcissism to hide the effects of an abusive or traumatic childhood would have to be done with extreme caution.

Even if the issues are genetic, there is no straightforward way to treat genetics in the context of a learned behavior cycle. Hereditary behavioral issues are something that a species line has become accustomed to over time. Somehow, that particular genetic sequence has come to be regarded as more significant than others. Whether this has anything to do with the individual's biological mating habits or some kind of protective reaction on the part of the line, it is a fundamental aspect of who they are. Similar to how someone is more likely to have a stronger inclination to be a leader or work with people for a living, being someone who believes they are superior to others will likely be ingrained in their minds from an early age. This, like all learned behavior, is passed down from one or both parents. If the parent(s) share the same genetic disposition, they will raise the child in the same frame of mind, and the person will become trapped in a vicious cycle. Being genetically superior and being raised to believe they are will be the primary motivator for narcissists, which will be difficult to change. Victims may become so adept at teaching them to question, dismiss, or shove down their responses to toxic behavior that they may become unable to recognize a healthy relationship once they have been taught. The body can sometimes provide clarity when the mind is clouded by confusion. In this exercise, you will investigate how your body communicates whether or not a relationship is healthy. Consider a relationship that you believe is toxic. Bring a mental image of the other person, or recall a memory of a negative interaction you had with that person. Don't go back to the most painful memory you can recall. Instead, recall an upsetting but not overwhelming memory from your past. When you have the memory firmly implanted in your brain, proceed to answer the next question.

What Is Narcissistic Abuse And The Different Types

Narcissists have an almost limitless number of ways to abuse others. They use intimidation and abuse to keep people in line and ensure they get what they want. Even though toxic narcissists, in particular, prefer to abuse people for sport, most of the time, narcissistic abuse is opportunistic and occurs when the opportunity arises. Rather than as a tool, the narcissist employs it as a weapon against their victim. They aren't concerned with the outcome, but they aren't necessarily doing it to be maliciously mean-spirited or to intentionally hurt someone; the harm is simply collateral damage due to their attempts to manipulate the other person into doing what they want. Their ultimate goal is usually to obtain whatever they desire rather than to cause harm to others. In addition to being far too preoccupied with their own feelings to be concerned about hurting others simply for the sake of hurting them, narcissists are typically far more preoccupied with themselves than others. However, these manipulation techniques can cause serious physical or emotional harm to others if used against them. This is an exhaustive list, but it includes some of the most frequently employed abuse techniques.

Physical
Physical abuse is the most common, including any harmful act inflicted on someone. Physical abuse can be physical contact, such as hitting or slapping, or it can be more violent, such as pushing, shoving, or throwing objects. Physical abuse can also take the form of sexual assault or stalking.

Sexual

Narcissistic abusers are often very demanding and seductive to get what they want from their victims. They may make sexual demands or become extremely possessive over sexual activities. If you are being abused this way, it is important to know that it is not your fault and that help is available.

Narcissistic abusers often use sex as a tool to control their victims. They may demand sex from their victims in exchange for favors or access to the victim's resources. Sometimes, the abuser will use sex as humiliation or revenge against the victim. The abuser may also use sex to gain power and dominance over the victim.

Verbal/Emotional

Verbal abuse intends to break down the target into submission. It is frequently used to make the other person feel insecure simply because they do not feel worthy of anything else. Verbal abuse has many different forms that it can take. They are harmful and make the victim wonder if they are to blame or overreact.

Verbal abuse almost always occurs in private since no one else is around to hear or witness it, allowing the narcissist to deny its existence if necessary. Unfortunately, this also isolates the victim, as the victim feels they cannot reach out to others because there is no proof of what was said. Thus, verbal abuse may not often happen at first. Still, it eventually escalates to the point that it is a typical communication method—particularly in private.

The victims of verbal abuse frequently rationalize the abuse as an acceptable form of communication. However, it is still difficult for the victims to deal with it at the moment. They may not recognize that it is another form of control over the victim's situation.

There are several different types of verbal abuse, some of which are easier than others to identify. Here are several abuse patterns, as well as an example of what they may look like at the moment:

Name-calling: "Wow, you're such an idiot! You never learn, do you?"

Manipulation: "If you loved me, you would do this for me, even if you don't want to."

Demeaning comments: "Wow, you're such a typical girl. You can't even remember to get your oil changed in your car. No wonder it broke down again."

Condescending: "Hah, no wonder you always complain about struggling with your schoolwork. You can't even figure out how to double a recipe!"

Nonconstructive and Cruel Criticism: "Can't you do anything right? You're always able to bring down the mood with one stupid mistake, aren't you?"

Threats: "You won't like what happens if you do that." Or "I will kill myself if you ever try to leave."

Blame: "It's your fault; we never have any money for anything fun." Or "Look at what you made me do! I would never have done it if you had just listened."

Silent Treatment: Your partner intentionally avoids talking to you to make you miserable.

Not all verbal abuse can be tagged as narcissistic. You must look at the behavior's context, frequency, and spite (hatred/vengeance), since people often criticize, interrupt, blame, be sarcastic, oppose, block, or blame you, depending on the situation. You must assess the frequency of this behavior.

Bullying, name-calling, shaming, belittling, demanding, blaming, threatening, criticizing, getting violent, accusing, undermining, and orders are all verbal abuse.

Mental/Psychological

Emotional blackmail is common in today's society and can be found in almost every relationship. People have mastered making sensitive statements or displaying sensitive emotions to make their partner believe their partner was mistaken. Emotional blackmail is a type of manipulation that can include punishment, anger, threats, intimidation, or warning. Therefore, it is also known as emotional blackmail.

It is the act of convincing someone else that their perception of reality is distorted or inaccurate, known as gaslighting. Gaslighting is one of the narcissist's most effective manipulative tools. It is one of his most frequently used manipulative weapons. To make you doubt yourself, the narcissist will do so gradually until you are convinced that you cannot be trusted and the narcissist has complete control over your life. Because you may have so much self-doubt that you are no longer confident in your ability to make important decisions, you will rely more on your partner for guidance. This also increases your likelihood of remaining in the relationship because you will not believe that what you believe happened actually did happen. You will pay attention if the narcissist downplays the incident or tells you it was not what you believe.

Typically, this begins slowly, with the narcissist portraying your belief as if it were a harmless error on your part. For example, suppose you tell them that your car keys are on the key holder. They correct you a few minutes later by saying that they were actually on the counter, even though they were, in fact, on the key holder. It progresses gradually from there until the victim believes anything the narcissist says.

Each instance of gaslighting will follow a specific pattern: Something takes place. A narcissist can have a distorted view of what has occurred, such as believing that they were the victim of an argument they initiated or creating a distorted view that will fit their narrative, even if they know it is incorrect. The narcissist then manipulates the victim into believing his distorted version of reality. The narcissist then gets the victim to believe him.

Narcissists may try one of the following methods to gaslight you into submission:

- Withholding: The narcissist refuses to hear your side of things or pretends that your side of the story does not make sense.
- Countering: The narcissist directly counters or questions the victim's perception of what has happened, questioning if it is accurate.
- Diverting: The narcissist changes the subject and accuses the victim of misremembering.
- Trivializing: The narcissist makes the victim feel that what the victim says or feels is unimportant or delegitimizes them.
- Denying: The narcissist feigns having forgotten what has happened or denies anything the victim says, saying it is falsified or made up on purpose.

Financial/Economic

This abuse occurs when the abuser controls all or part of the victim's money or economic resources. This often gives the abuser power over the victim and can make it difficult for the victim to get by. Financial/economic abuse can also lead to other types of abuse, such as physical or sexual abuse.

Cultural/Identity

The narcissist, master of manipulation, frequently casts out bait to get his way. First, they will lull you into complacency, making you feel your relationship is stable and comfortable, only to bait you into inciting an argument. Often, the bait involves something you are sensitive about. For example, the narcissist may know that you are sensitive about being cheated on in the past. So, for example, the next time you are out, they may look at another person, intentionally appearing obviously interested in the other person. They may even flirt with the other person to make you feel jealous.

When you inevitably call them out, they will deny doing anything like what you insist on. They will say they had no interest in the other person and turn it into an argument about their insecurities. They have essentially tricked you into an argument. Then, when anyone asks, they will tell the world that you constantly accuse them of cheating when they have no interest in being anything other than a perfect partner.

This has allowed the narcissist to create a victim narrative after baiting you into acting irrationally. They will use that cast bait any time they can. They want to make you feel like you are irrational and abusive.

Chapter 2: Narcissistic Personality Disorder

NPD (Narcissistic Personality Disorder) is the proper medical diagnosis for someone who has narcissistic tendencies. A narcissistic personality disorder is a very real and insidious personality disorder. Unfortunately, there is no cure or medication to alleviate the symptoms, and the narcissist frequently rejects the only treatments available. True narcissistic personality disorder (NPD) is not something to be laughed at; however, it has become somewhat fashionable to label people when they exhibit any signs of vanity. Because of the nature of their disorder, those suffering from narcissistic personality disorder have a particularly dangerous personality type. They should always be approached with the same caution you would use when approaching a bear or other potentially lethal predator. Suppose it is necessary to achieve the desired result, while the narcissist may not physically harm you. In that case, they will absolutely attempt to mentally and emotionally kill you if that is what it will take.

Traits Of People With Narcissistic Personality Disorder

Ultimately, a narcissist's behaviors can be reduced into one of three categories: A lack of empathy, a propensity for grandiosity, and requiring attention. If you had to describe a narcissist in the fewest words possible, it would be "attention-seeking, grandiose, and lack of empathy." Though this is technically correct, one must meet at least five of nine criteria to diagnose NPD, as dictated by the fifth edition of the *Diagnostic and Statistical Manual of Mental Disorders* (DSM-5). In addition, the five behaviors must be pervasive, meaning they occur regularly and repeat in various situations. While it requires a minimum of five traits to earn a diagnosis of NPD, people with less than five traits could still toxically present enough to be a problem in your life. The nine traits of NPD are delusions of grandeur, an obsession with power and success, delusions of uniqueness, entitlement, manipulation, lacking empathy, envy, arrogance, and constantly requiring attention from others.

Grandiose
People with narcissistic personality disorder are often preoccupied with self-importance and exaggerate the importance of their accomplishments and abilities. They may also be egocentric and believe they are superior to others. People with this disorder often completely disregard other people's feelings and often see themselves as always right. They also tend to be very self-centered, believing they are the only person who matters in the world. A narcissistic personality disorder is a serious mental illness, and untreated individuals can become very destructive.

Obsessed With Fantasies of Success or Power

Because narcissists inherently believe in their own perfection through delusions of grandeur, they also believe they deserve nothing short of perfection. They feel that they deserve to get the perfect spouse because perfection deserves nothing less than perfection. They deserve the perfect house, the perfect vacation, the perfect job, the perfect family, and anything else they dream up. As the best person in the world as far as they are concerned, they deserve nothing less than the best, no matter how unrealistic or unattainable. They could convince themselves that they deserve to be the world's ruler and absolutely believe it.

Unfortunately for the narcissist, many of these desires are unattainable. Nothing in this world is perfect, although the narcissist may believe otherwise. Their delusions eventually become their downfall, as things frequently go wrong in the real world. Plans fail sometimes, people get short-changed, and perfection in the truest sense of the word is little more than an idea, a concept that people everywhere may strive for but never actually reach. Because perfection is impossible, the narcissist is never satisfied. They constantly feel their delusions of perfection challenged and often react poorly to such a slight. They become irate because things do not go their way, and nothing short of perfection is ever satisfactory.

Belief of Uniqueness

The narcissist views their inherent superiority as support for their desire to be different from everyone else. As a result of their perception of themselves as distinct from others, they believe that they cannot connect with others, which leads them to believe that they cannot connect with anyone else. Their individuality is used to justify other people's inability to comprehend them, particularly when others attempt to label them or their behaviors as delusional or bizarre. Someone uncomfortable with a decision they made takes comfort in that they can dismiss that person's point of view as coming from someone who is not intelligent, cultured, or informed enough to understand the workings of their own mind. Someone who is less eminent than they are will never be able to comprehend their innermost thought processes. As a result, any opinions expressed are worthless to them in the first place.

This belief that other people cannot possibly understand them is accompanied by the belief that they can ignore other people's displeasure. Suppose someone approaches them and expresses displeasure with what they have done. In that case, they can shrug it off and believe wholeheartedly that the other person cannot comprehend what they have done. Suppose they decide to fire someone who works for them. A coworker may come over to express their disappointment. They would respond by stating that they had plenty of good reasons to fire the person and that their judgment should not be questioned. They do not need to justify such a decision to anyone else and have chosen not to do so. As a result, they carry on with their business, as usual, believing that the displeasure of others is too insignificant to bother with.

In addition to this sense of being unique, narcissists are frequently seen refusing to associate with others they do not consider equally as unique, powerful, or intelligent as they are. Instead, they desire to associate with people they believe can understand their own thought processes, and anyone else is considered unimportant to them.

Entitlement

Narcissists often feel entitled to special treatment and privileges. They feel superior to others and believe they deserve admiration, love, and adoration. They also believe that they are not obligated to others or to any kind of moral code. Narcissists usually expect to mirror their own feelings and thoughts in others. They may be very demanding and have a high opinion of themselves.

Manipulative or Exploitative

Since narcissists' perception of the world is strongly distorted, they have to manipulate others to get what they want. They have mastered manipulating others to make them see what they see and do so convincingly. If someone dares to question their perception of reality, they will not hesitate to blatantly lie about the situation. They may even tell the other person that they are insane and imagining things, even though it is truly their own perception of reality that is skewed.

Narcissists even manipulate others with their personalities—they pretend to be perfect and present themselves in a confident, perfect manner, even though internally, they are quite broken and lack identities. They literally wear masks to skew people's perceptions of them in hopes of getting what they want. The narcissist is a master at doing so covertly, ensuring that the manipulation tactics can always be denied if necessary. If they are called out for these tactics, they will deny, deflect, and distract the accuser using any necessary means.

The narcissist will also not hesitate to take advantage of other people. They do not care who gets hurt unless they are harmed. Any other person being harmed or wronged is seen as little more than collateral damage that is not worth paying attention to or regretting. They will use people to get what they want, seeing them as little more than a means to an end, with no regard for what the other people end when they are done.

Lacking Empathy

Empathy is incredibly important in human societies. It is used to communicate wordlessly and understand how other people are doing to ensure their needs are met, even if someone has to help. When you can tell at a glance that your child is hungry, your empathy and understanding of what hunger feels like encourage you to act to provide your child with food to assuage that suffering. This is the basic concept of empathy. Understanding how other people feel as though you are feeling that particular feeling at the moment.

Narcissists lack this empathy. They can see other people's feelings but do not feel them themselves. Though the narcissist may look at you and see you crying, they do not care that you are unless your tears stain their clothes or prevent you from doing whatever they want or expect from you. You may have just lost someone and are grieving that loss is irrelevant to them. This is why narcissists have no qualms about using others—they do not feel the pain of being manipulated. While they can see that there is pain involved, they do not feel that pain upon looking at the person who has been wronged simply by looking at them. That pain is a good deterrent for people who can feel empathy—pain and guilt kick in, causing them to stop.

Envious or Believing Others Are Envious of the Narcissist

Because narcissists believe they deserve the best, they frequently look at other people and feel jealous when they see someone else with what they have. If they apply for a job, but someone else gets it, they will envy the other person. If someone else obtains the girl they desired, they will be envious. If someone were to win the lottery, they would envy their good fortune. They will try to avoid the person they envy, never expressing their gratitude to the other person.

On the other hand, they will take their envy and attempt to deflect them onto the other person, which is known as a deflection tactic. As a result, the other person's newfound achievement or success may be downplayed. They may turn the situation around to claim that they should be envied.

Consider the scenario in which the narcissist was passed over for a new promotion, for example. They may argue they were fortunate not to receive the new promotion because the new position came with many additional responsibilities. The slight pay increase did not compensate for the additional workload. Their argument would be that not receiving a promotion is unquestionably the better situation to be in and that the person who did receive the promotion will be so busy that he will never have time to see his family because he will have to stay behind at work for longer periods now to ensure that everything is completed. As an alternative to stating that they are envious of the other person, they present the situation so that the person who did receive the promotion should be envious of them.

Arrogant

Narcissists are often very arrogant and believe they are superior to others. They have an inflated opinion of themselves and may be unwilling to recognize the accomplishments or worth of others. They typically view others as objects or sources of gratification, rarely caring about other people's feelings. Narcissists often expect special treatment and a level of deference that is not warranted. Because they are so self-centered, narcissists find it difficult to form close relationships with others.

Constant Need for Admiration

Finally, narcissists thrive off of attention and admiration. They feel the need for these incessantly, and that particular attention they yearn for is referred to as narcissistic supply. The narcissistic supply comes from others fawning over the narcissist and positive attention.

Signs Of Narcissism in a Relationship

It is not easy to be in a relationship with a narcissist. The negative impact spreads to all aspects of your life, affecting everything from your ability to focus at work to your emotional and physical health.

Suppose your partner exhibits 5 or more of these signs. In that case, you are most likely in a relationship with a narcissist (also known as someone with a narcissistic personality type); or, in extreme cases, if you are in a relationship with someone who exhibits all of these signs, they will most likely have Narcissistic Personality Disorder or "NPD."

They Want To Be At The Center Of Everything

Have you ever tried to talk to someone who is "all about me"? Someone who only listens to themselves? Every conversation will be hijacked and redirected back to them, which will be noticeable.

Narcissists constantly seek attention; if this need is not met, they become irritated and resentful. Being in a relationship with a narcissist means that every decision, opinion, thought, goal, and choice (e.v.e.r.y.t.h.i.n.g.) is about them.

A sense of entitlement is part of the all-about-me syndrome. This can come across as "my way or the highway" in relationships, where your thoughts, feelings, and opinions aren't considered val Narcissist with NPD believes that the world revolves around them and that they are entitled to constant, excessive attention and admiration, as well as having everything their way.

They Are Very Charming At First

You will experience the highest highs you have ever experienced when dating someone early in the relationship. You will be spoiled, pampered, and showered with love and flattery. You will feel like the luckiest person on the planet and wonder, "How did I get so lucky?" and "Is this person real?" Narcissists are experts at using their charm to get what they want.

29

According to Michael Dufner and others' research, narcissists are attractive short-term romantic or sexual partners. They discovered that narcissists' mate appeal stems from their physical attractiveness and social boldness – displays of characteristics such as confidence, charm, and charisma.

However, as with anyone putting on a show, there is only so long you can keep up the act before your true colors begin to show. And the narcissist's act is no different.

They Don't Respect Your Boundaries

People with narcissistic tendencies deliberately disregard the boundaries of others. They frequently overstep the mark and use others without regard for the impact they may have on them.
The narcissist disregards other people's boundaries in various ways, including breaking promises or obligations regularly, borrowing items or money without returning them (with no intent to ever return or repay), and showing little remorse and blaming the other person when they have overstepped the mark.

You Are Alone

Isolation is common for a narcissist to gain control in a relationship. This control feeds their desire to have their way with everything and to have their partner become completely dependent on them.

A narcissist can isolate you b cutting you off from friends and family; controlling and monitoring your use of social media and phone calls; controlling your use of vehicles; pulling you away from hobbies; and, in some cases, disengaging you from the workforce, giving you complete financial control.

"Why do you bother spending your time and effort on her when you don't even like her?" or "I paid for this car, so of course, I get to say when you can use it," or, "I thought you loved me? "Why do you put in so many hours at work?"

Hearing constant put-downs, doubts, and jealous comments eventually leads to giving up everything that gives you your own identity. You devolve into a diminished version of yourself that you no longer recognize. Someone who has been molded to fit the narcissist's lifestyle and needs.

They Ignore Your Emotions

The need to be understood and freely express your feelings, desires, aspirations, and needs with your partner is an important part of any relationship.

Because of the narcissist's need to be wanted may appear caring and truly want what's best for you; however, the harsh reality is that they are more concerned with "what's in it for me?"

The narcissist will make decisions that benefit them rather than those that benefit (or harm) their relationship. They simply cannot understand your feelings because they are preoccupied with their own.

They Have A Short Temper

As previously stated, the narcissist believes that everything revolves around them and that their way is the only way. Therefore, when things don't go their way, they don't get all of the attention, or when someone disagrees with them, it's like walking into a lion's den. As a result, they struggle to regulate their emotions and behavior, deal with criticism and are easily hurt.

Narcissists can become impatient or angry when they do not receive the "VIP treatment" they believe they are entitled to.

They Don't Let You In

The narcissist has built an underlying current of insecurity, fear, anxiety, and shame beneath the wall to keep themselves above others. They will not tear down this wall because they need to feel superior.

Allowing others in and being truly vulnerable would be too risky, so they project a false sense of self-esteem and bravado and keep people at arm's length. This can be a dangerous game of cat and mouse in intimate relationships, with the narcissist constantly baiting for attention and pushing away when you get too close.

They Don't Take Responsibility

When you're in a relationship with a narcissist, you'll notice they're quick to take responsibility – especially when things are going well. The narcissist's ego is fed by credit, praise, positive and good.

You will never see or hear a narcissist take responsibility when something goes wrong. Instead, in these situations, they will blame, deflect, avoid, and deny, genuinely believing it had nothing to do with them and acting hurt that someone could even suggest it was their fault in the first place.

They Are Very Envious

Power, status, beauty, success, class, and status are common obsessions for people with narcissistic personalities. They are envious of those who have what they desire. On the other hand, narcissists may accuse others of envying them, including their own partners.

The critical point here is that how a narcissist appears on the surface is not the same as how the narcissist feels deep down inside. The narcissist has two selves at work: their authentic self (the one experiencing jealousy) and the fraudulent, fantasy self they try to sell to the public (the egotistical self-accusing others of being jealous of them).

Signs Of Narcissistic Parenting

A narcissistic parent is someone who experiences, is possessive of, and/or engages in marginalizing competition with their children. Typically, the narcissistic parent sees a child's (including adult children's) independence as a threat and coerces the offspring to exist in the parent's shadow with unreasonable expectations. The child is rarely loved simply for being themself in a narcissistic parenting relationship.

Tries To Live Through Their Child

The majority of parents want their children to succeed. However, some narcissistic parents set expectations not for the child's benefit but for fulfilling their selfish needs and dreams. Instead of raising a child whose own thoughts, emotions, and goals are nurtured and valued, the child becomes merely an extension of the parent's personal desires, with the child's individuality diminished.

Marginalization

Some narcissistic parents see their children's potential, promise, and success as threatening their self-esteem. As a result, a narcissistic mother or father may make a concerted effort to humiliate the child to maintain the parent's superiority. Nitpicking, unreasonable judgment and criticism, unfavorable comparisons, invalidation of positive attitudes and emotions, and rejection of success and accomplishments are examples of competitive marginalization.
"There's always something wrong with you" and "You'll never be good enough" are common themes in these insults. The narcissistic parent benefits from the offspring's lack of confidence by boosting their own insecure self-worth.

Feel Superior

Many narcissistic parents have a distorted self-image, with an arrogant view of who they are and what they do. Individuals around the narcissist are frequently treated as tools (objects) to be used for personal gain. Some narcissistic parents' children are objectified similarly. In contrast, others are taught to have the same false superiority complex: "We're better than they are." However, this sense of grandiose entitlement is almost entirely based on superficial, egotistical, and material trappings at the expense of one's humanity, conscientiousness, and relatedness. Being less human makes one more "superior."

Enjoy Flaunting

Many narcissistic parents enjoy showing others how "special" they are, which is closely related to grandiosity. They enjoy flaunting their superior dispositions, whether material possessions, physical appearance, projects and accomplishments, background and membership, contacts in high places, and/or trophy spouse and offspring. They go out of their way to gain attention and flattery.

For some narcissistic parents, social media is a magical place where they can constantly brag about how wonderful and envy-worthy their lives are. The underlying messages could be, "I am/my life is so unique and interesting," or "Look at ME – I have what you don't!"

They Are Inflexible

Certain narcissistic parents are extremely strict about their children's expected behaviors. They control their children in minor details and can become agitated if there is a deviation. On the other hand, some narcissistic parents are also sensitive and easily irritated. Reasons for irritation toward a child can range from the child's lack of attention and obedience to perceived flaws and shortcomings to being in the parent's presence at the wrong time, and so on.
The desire to control the child is one reason for the parent's inflexibility and touchiness. When narcissists see that the offspring will not always be pulled by the strings, they react negatively and dis proportionally.

They Lack Empathy

One of the most common manifestations of a narcissistic father or mother is the inability to be mindful of and validate the child's own thoughts and feelings. Only the parent's thoughts and feelings are important.
Over time, children exposed to this type of parental influence may respond with one of three survival instincts: they may fight back and defend themselves. They may flee to get away from their parent (s). Some people may begin to freeze and replace their invalidated real self with a false persona (playing a role), thereby adopting narcissistic traits.

Dependency/Codependency

Some narcissistic parents expect their children to be their caregivers for the rest of their lives. Dependence can be emotional, physical, and/or financial. While caring for elderly parents is an admirable trait, the narcissistic parent typically manipulates an offspring into making unreasonable sacrifices, with little regard for the offspring's own priorities and needs.

Chapter 3: Habits Of A Narcissist And How They Control People

The Different Types Of Narcissists

Today, narcissism is a topic that is frequently discussed. But unfortunately, people use the terms narcissist and narcissism casually, without considering what they mean by these terms. In reality, these terms have taken on a life of their own in contemporary culture, and their meanings may differ slightly from the traditional psychological concept. Currently, "narcissism" can be used as an insult or even a subtle dig to describe someone, particularly celebrities.

Classic Narcissists

Individuals classified as classic narcissists include those who are grandiose, exhibitionist or have high levels of functioning. They are the most fundamental definition of a narcissist. They are the type that comes to mind whenever the subject of narcissism is discussed. These are individuals who believe they are too good for everyone else while at the same time harboring a burning desire for everyone else to elevate them to a higher level of importance (Casale, Fioravanti, and Rugai, 2016).

Classic narcissists are people who seek attention. The majority of their conversations are peppered with anecdotes about their accomplishments. They believe they deserve special consideration and treatment due to who they are or what they have accomplished in life. Unfortunately, like many others of their kind, most of their stories are full of half-truths.

Just as much as they enjoy being flattering themselves, they also enjoy being flattering others. It is a boring avenue (a channel for pursuing the desired object) for a classical narcissist when no one pays attention to their actions.

They believe they are entitled to something, and if they do not receive it, they are dissatisfied. On the other hand, a classic narcissist will despise the idea of sharing the limelight with anyone else. therefore, if necessary, they will g

Vulnerable Narcissists

Vulnerable narcissists also identify as closet victims, compensatory or fragile narcissists. This category is for narcissists who don't like attention but still feel better than everyone else. Thus, instead of seeking attention like classical narcissists, they prefer to intertwine their lives with others (Hart, Richardson, and Tortoriello, 2018).

One of the common traits of vulnerable narcissists is to play the pity card. Their attention comes when they present themselves as wounded individuals who need to be cared for. Some vulnerable narcissists are too generous with people around them so that you don't forget who they are or what they did for you. What they need is admiration and attention to boost the image of their perceived worth.

Malignant Narcissists

Malignant narcissists are the most dangerous type of narcissist. They are shockingly reckless and destructive, often breaching social norms without regard for others. In addition, they often lack empathy and can be highly abusive.

Malignant narcissists typically start out as people who are charming and successful. Still, their need for admiration eventually overtakes their ability to think rationally or care about the well-being of others. As a result, they may have a seemingly perfect family life but can be incredibly damaging behind closed doors.

Overt and Covert Narcissists

Overt narcissists are the ones who are loud and proud about their self-centeredness. They're the ones who brag about their accomplishments and who will often put themselves first in everything they do. Covert narcissists, on the other hand, are quieter and more subtle in their self-promotion. They may not come across as overly self-involved, but they still valorize themselves   excessively.
Covert narcissists tend to be very charming and manipulative. They know how to get what they want, whether manipulating others into giving them what they want or getting what they need by appealing to their ego. They can be very convincing, so it can be difficult to spot them early in a relationship.
Often people with covert narcissism will start off by being very supportive and altruistic towards their partner. But eventually, they will start to take advantage of their partner somehow, whether that means demanding too much attention or using them for personal gain. Because covert narcissists are often very good at hiding their true feelings, it can be difficult for their partners to know when they're being taken advantage of.

Somatic and Cerebral Narcissists

Somatic narcissists focus on their body and how it functions. They may be preoccupied with their weight, appearance, or sexual prowess. Cerebral narcissists are more concerned with their intellect and status. They may be boastful or arrogant and view themselves as superior to others.

Inverted Narcissists

Inverted narcissists have a great deal of self-esteem and an intense need for admiration and validation. They are often very charismatic, which can be a major advantage in achieving their goals. They often have a grandiose sense of self-worth and believe they are above the law and immune to criticism. In fact, inverted narcissists may even believe they are superior to others in intelligence, skills, or morality.
They often exploit others, either intentionally or unintentionally, believing they can get away with anything because they are considered superior.

How Does A Narcissist Control Others?

Narcissistic people are cunning, calculating, and often ruthless. They know how to use their charms, charisma, and intelligence to get what they want from you. And while they might seem like they have your best interests at heart, they're only interested in themselves. This article explores how narcissistic people control and manipulate you, what you can do to resist them, and the long-term consequences of letting them have their way.

Gaslighting

Narcissistic people use gaslighting to control and manipulate their victims. Narcissists claim that everything their victims say and do is wrong, even if it's the truth. They make their victims doubt themselves, making them feel crazy or stupid. Narcissists also make their victims doubt the reality of what happened, making them question their memories and senses of reality. This makes it hard for the victim to figure out what's true and what's not.

Projecting Negative Feelings On You

Narcissistic people often use projection as a way to control and manipulate others. They will try to blame their feelings or behaviors on someone else, even if that person doesn't actually do anything. This can make it difficult for you to deal with the Narcissist's behavior because it feels like you're always being blamed. Here are five common ways Narcissists project their negative feelings onto others:

- They accuse you of being insensitive or cruel.
- They say you don't understand them or care about them.
- They claim you're always trying to hurt them.
- They say you're never there for them when they need you.
- They say you never give them a chance.

Misrepresent Your Thoughts And Feelings

Narcissistic people commonly misrepresent your thoughts and feelings to manipulate you. For example, they may claim that you support their ideas or opinions when you really don't or that you agree with them when you really don't. In some cases, they may even make you feel like you're the only person who thinks this way or feels that way about them. This manipulation can be incredibly damaging and leave you confused, uncertain, and alone. On the other hand, suppose you are being manipulated by a narcissistic person. In that case, it's important to remember that they only do this to control and manipulate you. You don't have to let them do this to you – there are ways to break free from their grip.

Smearing And Stalking

Narcissistic people often smear and stalk their victims to control them. They use tactics such as spreading lies and rumors, monitoring their conversations and movements, and creating false online identities to attack and discredit their targets. As a result, victims of narcissistic abuse regularly feel like they are under constant surveillance and fear for their safety.

Triangulating

Triangulation is when someone uses the power of three to control and manipulate an individual. For example, narcissists use this strategy to isolate their victims from friends, family, and the support system that would otherwise help them deal with narcissistic abuse.

The triangulation strategy starts with narcissists using three different people to get information about their victims. These people can be friends, family members, or romantic partners. Narcissists use these people to get information about the victim's thoughts, feelings, and habits. They also use these people to try and gain trust and confidence to later manipulate the victim.

Once narcissists understand their victims well, they begin to use triangulation to control and manipulate them. Narcissists will use these people as pawns to get what they want from the victim. They will often use these people to embarrass or hurt the victim. Narcissists believe that by controlling and manipulating these people, they will be able to control and manipulate the victim's actions.

Sugarcoating And Baiting

Narcissistic individuals use a variety of tactics to control and manipulate others. One of the most common is sugarcoating their severe behaviors or negative comments to get you to react in a way that benefits them. For example, if your narcissistic partner constantly slams doors, they might say, "I just wanted to see if you were okay." This subtle tactic is designed to bait you into reacting and providing reassurance.

Another common manipulative tactic is baiting you with positive comments or rewards to get you to do something the narcissist wants but doesn't actually need. For example, suppose your narcissistic partner asks for your opinion on something important. In that case, they might offer to give you a coAgain later. Again, this could be a bribe to get you to agree to do something you would otherwise refuse.

These tactics are designed to create a sense of dependency in you and weaken your resolve. They know that when you're dependent on the narcissist, it's much easier for them to control and manipulate you.

Preemptive Defense Posturing

Narcissistic people often control and manipulate others by using pre-emptive defense posturing. This entails setting up a pattern of behaviors that the narcissistic person believes will ward off potential criticism or harm. The goal is to make the other person believe there is no way they could hurt or upset the narcissist, so they'll be less likely to do so.

This tactic can be effective in some cases, but it can also backfire if the other person doesn't fall for it. If they do, they may become caught in a cycle of constantly accommodating the narcissist's demands. They may also start to doubt their judgment and beliefs, making them feel more undervalued and insecure. If you're feeling manipulated by a narcissistic person, it's important to remember that you're not alone. There are steps you can take to regain control and heal your relationship.

Creating Conflicts

Narcissistic people thrive on drama and conflict, so they try to create as many as possible to control you. First, they will use arguments and accusations to get you upset, then use your emotions to manipulate you. This can be especially effective if you're insecure or have low self-esteem.

They know how to control your emotions and make you feel guilty or ashamed. They may tell you that you're the only one who can help them or that they love you too much to let you go. They may threaten to leave or hurt you if you don't comply.

They can also be incredibly possessive and will use any means possible to keep you under their thumb. They may refuse to compliment you or respond positively to anything you do. Or they may stop spending time with you altogether if they feel like you're no longer

Nitpicking Every Single Detail Of You

Narcissistic people are masters of controlling and manipulating others. They know how to get under your skin and use this knowledge to their advantage. Here are five ways narcissistic people control and manipulate you:

Constantly putting you down: Narcissists love to tear others down, especially those they view as weaker or inferior. It's a way of showing power and control over you. If you're always feeling down about yourself, it's difficult to stand up to the narcissist!

Making you feel like you're the only one who matters: Narcissists make you feel like the only person in the world that matters to them. They may tell you that nobody else understands or cares about you, which can lead to feelings of insecurity and isolation.

Silencing your opinions: Narcissists love to dominate conversations and shut down dissenting opinions. This way, they can control the information you hear and what impressions you form about the situation.

Manipulating your emotions: Narcissists know how to play on your emotions to get what they want from you. They may, For example, you feel guilty or bad.

Chapter 4: How To Deal With A Narcissist

How Would You Recognize A Narcissist?

Despite just how desperately narcissists want to believe they are unique, they are actually quite predictable. There are several traits and behaviors that a large majority of narcissists exhibit, and understanding these patterns will enable you to spot the narcissist from a distance, preferably before they can get close enough to you to do any real damage.

Controlling

Narcissists are controlling by nature. Because they seek to manipulate others into believing they are someone they are not, they seek to micromanage everything around them. The narcissist will desperately attempt to control you, using guilt tactics, abuse, and anything necessary to keep you in line. They will want to ensure you are only with people they approve of, doing things they are okay with, and acting in ways that will benefit them and them alone. If you are invested in anyone else, you are no good to them, so they seek to control your world until they are your world. That control allows them to also manipulate how you see the world, making you more likely to fall for their tricks in the future.

Critical

Because narcissists inherently have some fragile self-esteem and are terrified of failure or anything less than the best. They tend to be particularly critical of other people. Disparaging comments allow narcissists to feel better about themselves, particularly when they are already feeling sensitive or self-conscious. They will seek to tear down other people without any real advice that could put the other person in a position to fix things, and they seem to revel in it. This also allows them to constantly shift standards with partners. Suppose they can constantly find something to complain about. In that case, the other person is likely to try harder in the future to satisfy them, particularly with relationships. Suppose they do not like the food you cooked, for example. In that case, they may put it down, saying that someone else they know can make it so much better than you did in hopes that the shame would motivate you to try harder in the future. The entire purpose of this criticism is to leave the other person feeling insecure or as though they cannot do anything right.

Devil's Advocate

The devil's advocate, in an argument, is the one who takes the opposite side simply for the sake of the argument. This person may not necessarily believe what they are saying. Still, they tout the unpopular opinion anyway, preferably for intellectual discussion and to ensure that things are considered from all sides. However, the narcissist does not argue to find flaws. The narcissist does it to hurt the other person.

Narcissists love to cause chaos as chaos invites insecurity and uncertainty, both of which allow the narcissist to take command of the situation. The narcissist thrives off this and plays the devil's advocate to make it happen artificially. For example, suppose you have argued that everyone should get vaccinated and cited modem medicine as the reason for it. In that case, the devil's advocate may suddenly chime in with, "what if vaccines are a conspiracy by the Russians to make the US population weaker and therefore unable to fight them off?" The position is ridiculous, conspiratorial at best, and completely out of the left field.

Knowing That You Are In A Narcissistic Relationship

A narcissist is someone who loves themselves a bit too much. They're often very charismatic and make you feel like you're the most special person in the world. Narcissistic abuse can be highly manipulative and gradual, making it hard to recognize the issue.

If you've tried to end your relationship with a narcissistic partner, only to have them convince or manipulate you back into staying, then this post has been written for you. There are many common traits of narcissists. These are warning signs of gaslighting, abuse, codependency issues, or poor self-esteem. Read on to find out if your narcissist is abusing you.

The following are common traits of narcissists and abuse:

It's All Your Fault

A narcissist will blame you for the problems in the relationship, often shifting responsibility onto you so they don't have to take any blame for anything. They will always be right and never wrong, while you can do no right in their eyes. Always being at fault means you are less likely to pull away from them or confront them about their behavior because pointing out the truth could mean being abused further or being accused of being blamed for something else.

Controlling

Narcissists are control freaks. They have to control everything, often because of underlying insecurities. They are So putative when you don' They make you feel inadequate as if you can never meet expectations. The gaslighting will begin subtly by making little comments or suggestions to steer your behavior their way rather than what you want to do for yourself or your own needs. This could be anything from deciding how and when they come round to where and when you go on holiday together as a couple. A narcissist needs to be in the driving seat.

Extreme Jealousy

Narcissists are extremely jealous; this is just one of the many ways they try to maintain control over you. They will scrutinize your behavior, check your cell phone or social media accounts regularly, and even search your car or bags if they don't trust you to go out without them watching you. Jealousy can be a sign that you are being monitored. In addition, the jealous person often tries to isolate their partner from anyone other than themselves, so they cannot have an unbiased opinion of what is happening within the relationship.

"An Innocent Bystander"

Narcissists are always the victim, and you have to be the villain in their eyes. They will accuse you of having affairs, of being lazy, and most commonly, they
will blame you for everything that goes wrong between the two of you. Even when your partner is at fault, they will deny it and accuse you of something else so that it is always your fault in their eyes.

Deception and Fraud

Narcissists are masters of deception. They often lie about their past, intentions, and other people's motives to manipulate you into believing everything is fine when it is not. For example, suppose the partner suspects that you have been unfaithful. In that case, they will lie about it and makeup stories to tell you about them- suspicions. They will lie convincingly by telling you that they know someone who told them that they saw you doing something inappropriate. They will make you doubt yourself and your memory.

Love Bombing

Initially, a narcissist will treat you like the most special person in the world and shower you with compliments, gifts, and attention. The love bombing makes you feel on top of the world like no one else can ever fulfill your needs like this partner. They will make you feel like the most desirable person alive. Once they have you hooked, they will try to isolate you from your family and friends, making this the only person allowed to be in your life.

Humiliation and Punishment

Narcissists don't like being criticized or called out on their behavior. They will
often accuse their partners of being cruel towards them or too critical of them for daring to state that their partner is abusive toward them. They will then try to humiliate you for calling them out on these things by trying to show how "unreasonable" or "heartless" you are being. It's all in the name of the relationship and preserving it. If you are calling out their behavior, it can be because you don't want to be abused further or because you want to protect yourself from having your self-esteem eroded further.

Controlling When They Are Away from You

Narcissists have a history of being controlling when they are away from their partner, often telling them to cut off contact with family and friends to get advice or help from outside sources, which could make them reconsider things like ending the relationship. You will be told that you overreact to what is going on, and you should just be happy that someone loves you.

Financial Abuse

Another sign of narcissistic abuse is the way they control your finances. For example, they may make excuses for why they need to keep your bank details and close your cards. Alternatively, they may take it upon themselves to pay bills without discussion and even lie about how much money they have in their accounts, asking you for
money instead. If a narcissist has money to spend, then it is almost always their decision whether to go out and get something nice for themselves or not. It is rare for them to spend money on anything for their partner other than themselves.

Constant Criticism

Your partner may criticize everything you do. They may habitually roll their eyes and give you negative feedback instead of praising you. Due to this, there will be little or no appreciation for all the efforts you put into things. The only time they will ever express appreciation is if your relationship is already in a good place, "a "good" location Everything that occurs outside of this is a coincidence. "They become dissatisfied with their "good" relationship and complain or criticize it. They will notice everything about you if you're in a good place for them. It's possible that they won't see anything at all if you're not in a good position. This makes it difficult to gain confidence in yourself because you begin to question whether the person who jumped on every opportunity to criticize is someone worth spending time with.

Narcissists use a variety of tactics to control and manipulate their intimate partners. We must learn what these things are and how to warn others about them to avoid falling victim to these types of manipulators in the first place.

Dealing With A Narcissist

Identify The Type Of Narcissist You're Dealing With

Narcissists are classified into two types: grandiose and vulnerable.

The grandiose narcissist is self-assured, craves attention, and is adaptable. Therefore, the best way to deal with grandiose narcissists is to bring them on early and give them a critical role. In contrast, vulnerable narcissists are passive-aggressive and have low self-esteem. Vulnerable narcissists are more introverted than grandiose narcissists. Reassure vulnerable narcissists to keep them focused and their emotions in check.

Respond Instead Of Reacting

It is tempting to react to the narcissist's manipulative tactics with shock, disbelief, anger, and even pain, but these reactions provide the narcissist with a much-needed supply.
When dealing with narcissists, keep your attention on the issue and don't allow for deflection or projection. Returning the focus to the issue eliminates the narcissist's ability to monopolize the conversation or change the subject. When responding to a narcissist, be intentional and mindful of your words, and learn phrases that can help disarm the narcissist when they try to engage.

Avoid Direct Confrontation.

Because narcissists are hypersensitive to criticism, calling them out is rarely beneficial and frequently leads to them spiraling out of control. You might even set off their narcissistic rage. So instead, if you must provide negative feedback, try to frame it as much as possible as a compliment and only provide small doses of feedback.

Demand Results Over Promises

Narcissists are excellent planners, but they rarely keep their promises. The most effective way to hold narcissists accountable is to confront their deception. Remind them of their commitment and how much everyone looks forward to seeing them (playing to their ego). Do not complete any requests until your request has been met.

Refocus Your Attention On Yourself

Narcissists thrive on attention; no amount will ever be enough for a narcissist. However, you can break the spell by focusing on your needs, goals, and desires. Remember that their perception of you does not define you. Take note of your personal strengths, use self-affirmations to boost your confidence, and make time for self-care.

Keep Conversations Brief

Narcissists excel at over-communicating and domineering the conversation. This manipulation gives them leverage because they don't give you enough time to make your point.
Keep the conversation as brief and focused as possible, and redirect it as much as possible. When the conversation becomes one-sided, end it and move on. Finally, it's critical to recognize that most narcissistic situations go unresolved.

Inquire If Their Request Appears Responsible

Narcissists can appear out of touch with reality, exhibit unusual and sometimes dangerous behaviors, "play games" with your emotions, or make ridiculous and far-fetched suggestions. For example, they may ask you to co-sign on a car loan even if they are unemployed, or they may ask you to buy a house with them even if they only work part-time.
Ask the narcissist if what they say or do makes sense when responding to these irresponsible requests. Create similar scenarios for them to respond to or remind them of a time when they disagreed with a similar situation or request. Giving a reasonable suggestion or alternative can sometimes persuade the narcissist to reconsider their irrational requests.

Establish And Maintain Clear Boundaries

People with Narcissistic Personality Disorder frequently cross boundaries. Because rules do not apply to them, they have no problem bending and breaking them. They do, however, cherish their own boundaries.

When dealing with these people, make it a point to establish and enforce boundaries. Declare unequivocally what you will and will not accept. Any crack in your foundation invites others to violate and push your boundaries. Stand up for yourself, re-establish your boundaries, acknowledge unacceptable behavior, and respond to their violations.

Remind Yourself That You Are Not To Blame

A narcissist may attempt to blame you for anything that does not go their way. Remember that boundaries are important, including limiting your involvement in their lives. You don't have to accept blame when they try to shift it to you.

Gently Call Attention To Their Misbehavior

Narcissists are frequently unaware of the harm they cause to others. As a result, their behavior appears normal, and they will blame others for their failures and mistakes.

Gently draw attention to the undesirable behavior. Because narcissists dislike being perceived negatively, they will quickly change their behavior to appear positive.

If You Have To Be Around Them, Pretend To Be Interested.

When dealing with a narcissistic boss or authority figure, it's sometimes best to pretend to be fascinated. You are not required to agree or disagree. "That sounds interesting," "Tell me more about that," or "How do you intend to implement that" are appropriate responses. If it's a narcissistic coworker, tell them you're extremely busy or, "I'd love to talk, but I have to get this done by the end of the day."

Recognize When You Need Assistance

Because narcissistic abuse can be subtle, determining if you are a victim can be difficult. It's easy to get caught up in a cycle of narcissistic abuse and feel trapped with no way out. Signs that you may need to seek professional help vary by relationship. Still, suppose you are experiencing self-doubt or questioning your worth. In that case, you may need to seek therapy from someone trained in identifying and helping victims of narcissistic abuse.
Recovery can be a long process, and finding a mental health professional can be difficult. Still, it is worthwhile to begin your healing journey.

When Is It Time To Leave?

Narcissists are skilled manipulators and deception masters. Gaslighting, belittling, love bombing, and projection are techniques used to maintain or control a relationship, even when working to end it.

If you feel out of sorts, confused, or unable to explain what is going on, it may be time to end the relationship. However, it is not worth losing sight of yourself or your self-worth to remain in a relationship that does not meet your needs. Narcissistic abuse syndrome can have long-term consequences for a person; avoid it by knowing when to leave.

Not every narcissistic relationship has the same dynamics. These can vary depending on the situation...

Suppose you're in a romantic relationship with a narcissist. In that case, they may constantly make you feel like you're "not good enough" and use gaslighting to keep you in the relationship.

If your mother or mother-in-law is narcissistic, she may compete with you, compare herself to you, or constantly portray herself as a victim.

When dealing with a narcissistic boss, they may appear entitled and demanding, and they may never give you positive feedback (but expect it from you)

If you know a communal narcissist, they may believe they are the best listener and giver while keeping as much attention on themselves as possible.

Chapter 5: Recognize and Stop a Narcissistic Abuse

Understanding The Cycle Of Abuse

The following steps are all a part of the narcissistic cycle of abuse. These happen in virtually every single cycle, so it is important to be cautious and aware. If you are a victim, pay attention to these cycles so that you can begin to witness them as they happen. This will support you in having a greater understanding of your abuser, seeing the reality behind what they are doing, and giving you the power to leave.

Idealize

The process of idealization enables narcissists to present themselves as better than they actually are in real life. During this stage, they frequently engage in what we refer to as "love-bombing." This means that the narcissist begins to construct an ideal relationship for you by lavishing you with interest, love, and affection. Because of this, you develop a strong sense of trust in the narcissist, which allows you to connect with them deeper— at least, that's what you believe. You share a lot with them, including your deepest secrets, hopes, and fears, and they get to know you better. They will also share information with you, though it is rarely genuine information. It is possible that this is not even the truth in many cases.

The narcissist will continue to play games with you for a while, making the relationship appear almost "too good to be true," but never let the other shoe drop on the other foot. At least, not until the appropriate time has come to do so. Instead, they allow you to become intimately acquainted with them. They give you enough time to develop strong feelings for them and see what a wonderful person they are—or, more accurately, what a wonderful person they want you to believe. Simply put, the connection and ecstasy that you two have shared are extraordinary. If you haven't already, you can't believe your luck in meeting someone with whom you can connect on a deeper level while also experiencing explosive physical chemistry. You just can't get enough of it.

During this stage, the narcissist is primarily concerned with gathering information. Everything you say to them is being recorded and stored to be used against you later on during the devaluation phase of the market. They want to create a safe environment for you so that you believe they have everything you desire. They want to know everything about you so that they can use that information against you in the future if necessary. As soon as they've hooked you, they know you'll do whatever it takes to keep the relationship alive. A key step in maintaining your emotional attachment to the narcissist for as long as possible is recognizing that they have done something wrong.

Devalue

When the narcissist is confident that they have gained a significant amount of control over you and that you have invested a significant amount of time and energy in the relationship, the narcissist will begin to move into the "devaluation phase." This is the point at which they begin to chip away at you and shift your perception so that your strengths are perceived as flaws instead of strengths. The transition from idealization to devaluation is a long and drawn-out process. Because it is so subtly disguised, you may not even notice it exists at first. They purposely bring it out slowly and deliberately, gradually increasing your tolerance for their abuse as they go. They may start with a lot of "pull" and a little "push," drawing you in and keeping you coming back to see what happens next.

The situation begins to shift, however, as time goes on. The 10 percent push will soon be followed by a 20 percent push, a 30 percent push, and so on until the entire relationship is filled with abuse and toxicity to most of the population. The gradual increase may take months or even years to reach maximum capacity. Everything from the length of time it can take to the amount of pressure placed on the victim is based on the signals you send out and your level of tolerance. The narcissist wants you to believe that they are winning, and they want you to believe that you are giving to them. Even if you have stronger boundaries going into the relationship or demand that the relationship starts with an even 50:50 power and control, they will apply the maximum amount of pressure you can handle without realizing what is going on until they win the battle.

On the other hand, you are the frog in the boiling water at that point. They have conditioned you by gradually increasing your tolerance over time. You were completely unaware of what was happening because it happened so gradually. Otherwise, you would immediately be alerted to the abuse and flee the scene. As a result, they strategically measure only what you can handle and continue pushing you further. Occasionally, they may have to throw you a lifeline in the form of flattery or affection to keep you on their good side. The primary goal is to shift the ratio from majority positivity to majority negativity and increase your tolerance level, gradually eroding your sense of self-worth. As your tolerance for the abuse increases, it becomes increasingly difficult for you to leave.

As soon as the narcissist believes that they have achieved a high enough push/pull ratio, they recognize that they have achieved a state of control. They begin to feel in control of the relationship, and things deteriorate rapidly. They begin to take advantage of the fact that they are now in command. The pressure increases even further, possibly causing the ratio to increase quickly now that they know you will not be leaving the company. This process stage will also include targeting other potential victims to lure them into the trap. As a result, when they reach the devaluation phase with you, they will be able to begin receiving attention from another source. The result is that they are constantly receiving attention while simultaneously grooming everyone else to give it to them.

The victim goes through a very painful and traumatic period during the devaluation phase of the process. If you were once thought to be self-assured and sexy, people would trick you into believing you are cocky and self-centered. If you were once intelligent, you have now descended into the status of "know-it-all." In the devaluation phase, they will gaslight you, invalidating your feelings and beliefs while coercing you into believing a false reality far from the truth. You will begin to have your self-image and sense of self-worth shattered. Your accomplishments become meaningless as you become discouraged and filled with feelings of doubt, fear, and insecurity. In the devaluation phase, your ability to create future success is limited. You are filled with a sense of insecurity that makes it seem like you have no way out. Due to the narcissist's desire to destroy you in every way possible, this stage of the abuse cycle can be extremely traumatizing.

During the devaluation phase, most victims have no idea what they are experiencing. They do not know what they are going through. Victims are entangled in a web spun by the narcissist, and they often have no idea they are even in it. It is extremely painful when in this stage. The heart-breaking thing is that the victim will do everything to fight to get back to the initial love-bombing phase of affection, chemistry, connection, ecstasy, and love. But it is too late. This is exactly where the narcissist wants you.

From here, the narcissist will do one of two things. First, they will move back and forth between the idealization and devaluation phase if they are unsure where you stand and how deep you are in the hole. The devaluation phase will grow longer and longer each time until, eventually, you are there almost permanently. At that point, you will only be entered into the "idealization phase" as a reward for your behavior if they feel that you deserve it. That way, they continue to give you small reasons to stay with them, which you will cling to due to your internal emotional, and mental destruction.

This enforces your codependency and allows them to slowly but consistently hack into your self-confidence, self-esteem, and self-worth. At this point, you are still desperately clinging to the initial love-bombing phase, and the idea of leaving the relationship is more painful than tolerating the abuse. However, once they are confident that you are officially hooked and can treat you in any way they want, they will begin, including the "discard phase."

Discard

The narcissist will discard you during your desperate attempts to return to the initial phase that felt so good. Because you feel deeply insecure and insignificant, they know that you will do anything to seek their approval. This essentially conditions you to seek excessive admiration from the narcissist, putting the power directly in their hands. Now, they use your need for validation to support their own agenda. They will frequently withdraw, telling you that everything you have done for them is a sign of failure and blaming you for not making them feel "good " That way, you begin to blame yourself. As you continue to seek validation desperately, they use all of your attempts as a way to feed and fuel their own need for validation, attention, praise, and admiration. In other words, you are feeding the fire.

This behavior supports the narcissist in scooping out all the remaining qualities within you that do not serve their agenda. At this point, they know that you are so desperate for their attention and affection that you will do nearly anything to win it back. So, they scoop it away. They know that there is a good chance that you have not even yet begun to realize how minimal your self-esteem and self-worth have gotten because the devaluation has been so slow and gradual. To them, this means that you are oblivious to what keeps you attached, which means there is little chance that you can or will break the attachment. You may grow frustrated and leave for some time, but this rarely lasts. You would first have to recognize what was going on and then receive help to leave the situation permanently, which is an unlikely scenario for most victims. At this point, nothing you can do will fill their high standards. Instead, they set their standards higher and higher, continually putting them out of reach so that you cannot possibly achieve them. As the blame-shifting continues, they will use your desperation and confusion as an opportunity to turn themselves into the victim. Often, they will blame you for what they have done themselves and then delude you into believing that you actually did it.

As this happens, the narcissist will bring other people into the dynamic. They will bond with other victims during your time apart to fill their needs and create a love-bombing phase. In their mind, they are creating backup plans of narcissistic supply just in case you manage to escape forever. The narcissist cannot cope alone. When you get back together with the narcissist, they will claim that this person is close to them but has no impact on your relationship. They will then successfully keep two or more of you trapped in this cycle, constantly switching between which one has the "pleasure" of filling their needs. The narcissist will rarely, if ever, spend time alone during these discard phases. Even being alone for as little as a few nights is enough time for triangulation to root in deeply and start, especially because the narcissist has already been priming their next victim since the devaluation in most phases.

How To Get Over Narcissistic Abuse Quickly

If you are currently living with Narcissistic abuse recovery, you have probably done a lot of research to find some answers. You've likely been told again and again by well-meaning family and friends that time heals all wounds, but that sounds like a really long time to wait for the pain to go away.

Here are a few hints for how to get over Narcissistic maltreatment quicker:

Step 1: Commit to Repentance Immediately - Soon, Not Later!

Repentance and healing are absolutely necessary to get over Narcissistic abuse sooner. You can't recover if you don't sincerely repent for the wrongs you have committed against yourself or others. Repentance is a religious term; however, it means that you sincerely regret your past behavior, with a desire for a change in behavior in the future. Healing cannot begin until the repentance process begins. The sooner you admit that your past behavior was wrong (instead of blaming others, hating them, grumbling about others, or making excuses), the sooner healing will begin, and you can get over Narcissistic abuse. If you don't acknowledge that whatever you did is wrong, how will you ever be able to stop doing it?

Step 2: Don't Give Up on Becoming Your Best Self - Even if You Fail a Thousand Times!

When we work on something repeatedly (like acquiring another expertise), it turns into a propensity, which is what we need with Narcissistic maltreatment recuperation! We want to become habitual at being our best selves. This takes time and practice, but with a little determination, there's no stopping you! You cannot move forward until you learn to have healthy boundaries and a healthy sense of self. You can't get over Narcissistic abuse if you're still suffering from the trauma of Narcissistic abuse. The more closely you follow the steps we will enumerate below, the sooner you'll be able to experience Narcissistic abuse recovery.

Step 3: Seek Out Support - But Avoid "Helping" People Who Don't Want It

You have most likely done a great deal of exploration to discover a few answers about Narcissistic maltreatment recuperation and how to get over it quicker. Did you ever use Google search in the form of "how do I get over narcissistic abuse faster"? If so, that's a good indication that you are ready to heal. That's great! We can help you get over narcissistic abuse faster with a few simple steps:
1. Step 1: Ask yourself a couple of questions.
2. Step 2: Do some research.
3. Step 3: Read this article thoroughly.

Most importantly, when somebody requests exhortation, they normally need guidance about self-imposing [that implies figuring out how to defeat their issues through training and willpower]. It's not their place to judge if you are providing the advice. When someone asks for advice, they typically want to know:
- Where can I get Narcissistic abuse recovery help?

- What products are available (books, online courses, etc.)?
- What is the best way to get over Narcissistic abuse faster?

Helpful answers will point them in the right direction. You see, gaming knowledge has nothing to do with helping people or giving them what they need... It's about directing them to solutions that will help them get what they actually want for themselves [what you want for yourself, too!].

Step 4: Don't Give Advice Unless Asked

Try not to offer guidance unless someone asks for it. You can help them find solutions to their problems when they ask. Tell them if someone asks you for advice, and you know the best way to overcome narcissistic abuse faster! Your duty as a caregiver to others is to give them the best advice possible to become the best possible version of themselves.

Step 5: Be Inspiring! Tell Stories That Will Help Others Get Over Narcissistic Abuse Faster!

You can inspire others in Narcissistic abuse recovery by sharing stories about your accomplishments. People want to know how you got over narcissistic abuse faster. If you don't share your personal stories, people will never experience the amazing things you accomplished in your life. You can start by telling them about how you overcame Narcissistic abuse earlier in your life— tell them all about it from the beginning of your recovery.

Step 6: Share How You Overcame Your Past - On Social Media!

Sharing what you have done with others will help them overcome narcissistic abuse faster when facing setbacks or failures. Sharing your stories about overcoming narcissistic abuse will inspire others. Furthermore, social media has a huge impact on your interpersonal relationships. Sharing your story with the help of Facebook, Twitter, and LinkedIn greatly improves the quality of your relationships in Narcissistic abuse recovery!

Step 7: Eliminate Your Negative Self-Talk - Because It Keeps You Stuck in the Past!

To get over narcissistic abuse faster, you must focus on leaving the past behind. You need to keep repeating how great you are now— because they'll start to believe it—and you also need to eliminate any negative self-talk that keeps you stuck in the past. Instead, you need to focus on how great you are today so that they will believe it.

Step 8: Don't Take Them to Extremes - Do the Best You Can!

Getting over narcissistic abuse faster is not about providing a perfect solution or an idealized lifestyle for people. It's about helping them find a solution to their problems when they need it most and then helping them practice what their new skills will enable them to do. They'll thank you for refreshing their minds and reminding them of how great their lives can be now!

Step 9: Avoid Self-Judgment - Don't Judge Them!

Don't try to judge the reason why someone is in Narcissistic abuse recovery. It's not personal. You couldn't possibly know why a person is in Narcissistic abuse recovery, and it's not your place to try to understand that. However, you can understand the negative impact of narcissistic abuse on the mind and body. That is enough to know that you need to help them overcome narcissistic abuse faster!

Step 10: Only Give Advice That Will Work - Acknowledge Their Struggle!

For other people to get over narcissistic abuse faster, they need someone who has been there and done that—someone who has experienced what they are experiencing now, who understands their struggles and pain. Give advice only if it will actually help them get over narcissistic abuse faster. Acknowledge their struggle, that they are in Narcissistic abuse recovery, and how much it will help them. All of your support can only benefit them!

Step 11: Help Them Fall in Love with the Process of Getting Over Narcissistic Abuse Faster - Help Them Fall in Love with Getting Over!

You've given them hope by encouraging them to get out of narcissistic abuse faster. Now, it's time to help them fall in love with the process—not just the outcome. First, you must show them how they can do it themselves to get over narcissistic abuse faster. Then, you'll feel great when you see their smile for yourself or hear about their success story if they tell you about it. And this is how you start helping them fall in love with the process of getting over narcissistic abuse faster.

Step 12: Help Them Fall in Love with Self-Care and Healing Techniques

Now, it's time to help them find the self-care and healing techniques for Narcissistic abuse recovery they need to get over narcissistic abuse faster. If you guide them properly, you'll see that they develop new coping skills quickly. You'll be amazed at how much progress they make when you're in Narcissistic abuse recovery. This will also motivate them to keep going when it seems difficult or hopeless.

If you are supporting another person in narcissistic abuse, do your best to express yourself honestly and with compassion. Then, when you see that they are making progress, let them know how proud you are of them. This will give them the positive feedback they need to continue recovering from narcissistic abuse.

Chapter 6: Processing Your Trauma

Many people believe you cannot find love until you learn to love yourself. This is a common adage. Unfortunately, this is often the case for the majority of things. For example, after you have learned to be patient with yourself, you can teach others how to be patient with them. To be sure, you may already be more patient with others than yourself in certain situations. But, on the other hand, you'll discover that when you fail at being patient with others, it's most likely because you have no patience with yourself when making that particular type of mistake.

Someone in my family is always early to everything, which bothers me. That same family member has no patience for people who are late for appointments. I'm sure you have similar examples in your mind as well. The point is that when it comes to issues with which we are not patient with ourselves, we often have less patience for others. One way to cultivate patience with yourself is to reflect on your own intentions and the intentions of others.

We ask for forgiveness because our intentions were not to cause harm. This is a common occurrence. For example, you may express regret but did not intend to offend in the first place. What you're saying is that you had no intention of offending anyone. In this case, you express your regret and ask for forgiveness for your actions, stating that you did not intend to offend anyone in the first place. When you make a mistake, examine your actions to determine whether or not you intended to make a mistake. If you did, you might find yourself in a position where you must deal with yourself further. If you didn't, you might approach yourself the way you would approach someone else who had made an unintentional error. Alternatively, you could approach yourself the way you would want someone else to approach your unintentional mistake: gracefully.

I realize this is a strange train of thought. Being patient with others necessitates the development of patience with oneself. Being patient with oneself necessitates treating oneself with the same patience one treats others. I understand that it appears to be a contradiction. What it actually achieves, on the other hand, is the resolution of a contradiction.

A paradox is something that appears to be in opposition to one another but is not. For example, it appears contradictory that you would have to learn to be patient with yourself to be patient with others, given that you are naturally more patient with others. It isn't a contradiction in the traditional sense, though.

Therefore, if you apply your more natural disposition toward patience to yourself, you will be even more patient with others because you will have resolved those instances of complete inability to be patient with yourself. Thus, you'll be able to overcome your failures if you have patience.

Again, your failures regarding patience are almost always linked to the instances in which you don't allow yourself to be patient with yourself. Suppose you are unable to maintain your own patience during the delay. In that case, you will be unable to maintain the patience of others as well. This isn't necessarily a bad thing in and of itself. You could live a completely fulfilled life if you didn't have any patience for being late. The point is not that the subject is important.

Put another way, the more patience you demonstrate for yourself, the more patience you will demonstrate for others. As a result of your natural tendency to be more patient with others than yourself, practice patience with yourself. As a result of allowing yourself more patience, you will find more patience with other people. It's that simple or that complicated, depending on your perspective. In either case, you are capable of completing the task.

If you want to improve your patience with yourself, there are many activities you can engage in. This is critical to your ability to recover and build new relationships after a breakup.

In a narcissistic relationship, you must learn to protect yourself from being drawn into another. However, it is also important not to become so impatient with anything that reminds you of the narcissist from your previous relationship that you find it difficult to form new relationships.

In contrast to how the narcissist you were with made you feel, the world is more stimulating. You'll have to develop new activities to re-establish your presence in the world. Your relationship with a narcissist was destructive to your sense of self, boundaries, reality, and ability to control your actions. The most important thing you can do is actively participate in activities that will return you to a place where you can regain your sense of identity and self-control.

Your goal is to find activities that will allow you to reclaim what has been taken away from you. You'll want to re-establish your personal boundaries at some point. You'll want to reclaim your identity at some point. Find a relationship where reciprocation is easy to come by and is recognized as important to your happiness.

You already have the resources you need in your home, neighborhood, and backyard to reestablish your personal space. Make a concerted effort to regain control over your boundaries. You now have the resources you need to reclaim your identity. Make a concerted effort to develop your own sense of self. Recognize how your creativity has been stifled and how you can reclaim it.

For your recovery to be successful, you must first acknowledge that you have experienced a personal problem that has caused you to lose your sense of self. Then, you must get out into the world and re-discover your unique place. Finally, you must reclaim your life without the narcissist with whom you were previously involved in a relationship.

Yoga is a wonderful way to stimulate a fruitful connection between the mind, the body, and surroundings for people who may not be ready to participate in traditional sports or other strenuous activities due to health or physical limitations.

Your body's boundaries, as well as your mind's need for human connection and a sense of reality, were violated by the narcissist with whom you were in a relationship at the time. As a result, it is past time for you to engage in activities that help you reconnect with the earth and look inward once more.

Like yoga or anything else, mindfulness can be practiced and honed; all it takes is a conscious effort on the practitioner's part. After all, conscientiousness is synonymous with mindfulness. As soon as you begin doing activities for yourself again, you will notice an improvement in your mindfulness. Nothing more than doing the work to articulate your experience and give yourself the understanding that you are once again in control of your own destiny is required!

These activities are intended to provide you with ideas for triggering these experiences and inspiring the reclamation of one's identity. Make good use of them, but don't be afraid to invent your own adventures. The important thing is to get started as soon as possible and with diligence.

Your self-reflection will be prompted by your mindfulness/conscientiousness, you will discover. If you've wondered how anyone can teach self-reflection, you've come to the right place. You've asked a fantastic question. Some people appear to be withdrawn and inward. Those around them appear to be looking outward. However, we can all shift our gaze in different directions.

When you were in the company of a narcissist, you both looked into each other's eyes. After that, you should practice gazing inward toward yourself and then outward toward things other than the narcissist who convinced you that your gaze was most valuable when directed at them.

Self-awareness is a critical component of living a fulfilling life. Children become self-conscious during a frightening period of their lives. In a colloquial sense, we use the term "self-conscious" to describe someone shy or socially anxious in social situations. Its literal meaning is necessary to be self-aware and aware of one's own existence as an individual. Without much forewarning, any child will develop self-awareness and self-consciousness (both meanings are now applicable). When this occurs, they must understand how to self-reflect and communicate their self-reflections to others.

This is how we transition from turning inward to turning outward. You will learn to respect your self-awareness and ability to turn inward and outward. This is because you have been staring at the narcissist for a long time, which is unusual. It's time to turn your attention inward toward yourself and others.

Some people become entrapped in their inward selves. Numerous difficulties arise as a result of this. Relationships can be difficult as a result of this. It can make it difficult to maintain a stable job. It is critical to your recovery that you do not become trapped in a cycle of retreating within yourself or projecting outward without reclaiming your sense of self. The narcissist with whom you were conversing was hollow on the inside. They attempted to deplete your reserves as well. Don't make the same mistakes they did. You must look within yourself for the substance without losing sight of the fact that you must also look outside yourself, just as the narcissist struggled to do. These are the passages that you must write. You must discover who you are without becoming stuck in that place.

Nature walks will help you to expand your horizons. It will help you remember how to be more conscious of your own body and boundaries in the future.

You must take an active role in your recovery. Your abuse was received passively. It is now necessary to take action. Technology is the opposite of immediacy because it is a form of mediation between two parties. Technology serves as a middleman. Someone makes something specifically for us. We are not required to participate in the world on a direct basis. We'll be able to do it right away. We may not be able to speak with someone directly. Still, we can communicate with them indirectly through a social media application.

We can even spy on someone, making the experience more overtly indirect than it otherwise would be. Their lives and interests do not have to be known to us because we can sneak a peek into their lives and interests indirectly.

Overall, the author encourages more direct communication between you and your environment. These activities will continue to emphasize that you should actively consider yourself working toward your recovery every day that you are no longer in a relationship with a narcissistic personality disorder. So, of course, the first step is to determine whether or not this book is appropriate for you

Although you may have believed you were in a relationship with a narcissist, it is possible that the narcissist you were with was skilled at concealing their true nature at times.

The truth is that narcissists are very good at concealing what they are embarrassed about. They cannot cope with shame and do not want to experience it. They will avoid it at all costs. Those ashamed of their narcissistic parent may be particularly adept at hiding their true selves from those around them. You have to remember the unexpected outbursts and the abuse that you have endured in the past. Otherwise, you will never feel that you are reading the correct book.

Suppose you are sure by now that you were in a relationship with a narcissist, regardless of their ability to hide it from you occasionally. In that case, it is time for you to move towards acceptance of your abuse. Only once you accept the abuse can you move past it. It is time for you to acknowledge it and face reality like the narcissist could not.

Chapter 7: Starting Your Recovery Journey

Steps To Leaving A Narcissist

The fact is that a narcissist does not see the need to seek professional help because, after all, they believe that they are completely normal and unaffected by anything else in life. However, those who have been abused are encouraged to seek treatment. Suppose you have been or are currently in a relationship with a narcissist. In that case, you must end the relationship and seek professional assistance. Such assistance is essential in regaining self-confidence and self-esteem after a depression.

Believe me when I say you are far better than you could have imagined. Unfortunately, the narcissist may have succeeded in destroying your self-confidence and even your self-esteem. Still, the most important thing to remember is that you are simply a victim. You are not unworthy in the way that they would have you believe. Finding a health professional specializing in trauma recovery will assist you in your journey through the healing process and back to health and well-being. You can also seek a therapist's assistance if you cannot leave your abusive relationship. A therapist can teach you the most effective methods of communicating with your abuser so that you can set boundaries that they will respect and, thus, protect you so that they will no longer take advantage of you.

Here are some of the steps that you will have to go through to help you journey through healing to recovery:

Step 1: Cut Contact

Once you have left the relationship, keep it that way! Stop maintaining contact with your abuser. The main reason why you left is that the situation was not working for you. Therefore, there is nothing that will happen that can make things better. The best way to recover from abuse is for you to block all forms of communication. Unfortunately, suppose you have joint custody of the children. In that case, you may be unable to wipe this person entirely from your life. Therefore, it is advisable to create a strict custom contract. You only communicate on matters regarding your children and use third-party channels exclusively! Otherwise, ensure that you have set up court orders for all forms of agreements.

Think about the extreme trauma bonding, gross abuse, and addiction you had with the narcissist. Sometimes the best way is for you to accept that the only way you can recover from such damage is to pull away and cut your losses once and for all. Think of abstaining as a way of protecting yourself from hurt. In other words, each time you initiate contact with your abuser, you are handing them the ammunition to blow you off.

Remember that you lived with them, so they know your weak points and how they can wound you even more profoundly. It is not until we heal that we stop forcing ourselves toward the narcissist for loving or craving them or even justifying ourselves by giving them a second chance. When we completely stop contact, then we can begin to heal.

Step 2: Release That Trauma So That You Begin Functioning Again

If we are going to heal, we must be willing to reclaim our power. We must do the exact opposite of what we believed and say, "I can fix them. I will feel better." Your power belongs inside you. The moment you take your focus away from your abuser, then you will be able to channel that power into rebuilding your self-love and paying closer attention to making yourself whole again. At first, it might seem like understanding who a narcissist is and what they do is essential. But the real truth is that these things cannot heal your internal trauma. Instead, you need to decide to let go of that horrific experience so you can be at peace. You will begin to rise, get relief, and balance once you have decided to take your power where it belongs— inside you.

Step 3: Forgive Yourself for What You Have Been Through

When the insecure and wounded parts of ourselves are still in pain, we are frequently pushed into acting in ways similar to those of children who have been abused. The fact that we are constantly seeking approval from other people, especially from our abuser, gives us or her complete control over how we are treated. And it is at this point that you will realize that you have surrendered all of your resources to them, including your money, time, and health. The most unfortunate aspect of this is that, in the process, you end up hurting the people who are most important in your life: your children, siblings, parents, and other close family and friends.

While forgiving yourself for this may be difficult, it is necessary to rebuild your life and regain everything you have lost due to your abuser's actions. You will find resolution and acceptance sooner rather than later if you work through your healing process. Then, you can transform your life from one in which you lack self-love and respect into one in which you live with truth, responsibility, and well-being.

The moment you forgive yourself, you will recognize that this has all been a learning experience and that this is the lesson you have taken away from it. You will use this lesson to reclaim your life, as you will realize when you forgive others. When you let go of your regrets and self-judgments, you can begin to set yourself free to achieve greatness in your life, regardless of where you are in your life's journey.

The moment you begin to feel hope again is the moment that will propel you forward into fulfillment and a life filled with meaning.

Step 4: Release Everything and Heal All Your Fears of the Abuser

Do you know what bait to a narcissist is? Anxiety, pain, and distress. These things can perpetuate another cycle of abuse, no matter how we tell ourselves that we have separated from them.

It is indeed true that abusers can be relentless. In most cases, they do not like being losers. But one thing that you have to understand is that they are not as powerful and impactful as you may have thought they were.

They need you to fear and go through pain so that they can function. However, once you have healed your emotional trauma, they fall apart. Therefore, you must become grounded and stoic by not feeding into their drama; this way, they will soon wither away along with their power and credibility.

Step 5: Release the Connection to Your Abuser

There have been numerous instances where people likened their freedom from narcissism to exorcism. Liberating ourselves from the darkness that engulfed our beings allows us to detoxify and allow light and life to flow into our bodies. If the light has to take the place of the shade, the darkness must be expelled for something new to be welcomed in. In the same way, you must release all of the parts of yourself that have been imprisoned by your abuser to be able to access a more supernatural power—the power of pure creativity.

When you disentangle yourself from a narcissist, you are not only cutting the cord but also releasing all of the belief systems that you may have unconsciously associated yourself with during the relationship. Only then will you be able to break free from the illusion of being a new person and not a narcissistic target. Even though it may be tempting to seek retribution against your abuser, this is something that you must make a concerted effort to avoid doing. Rage can pull you back into deeper darkness and into a game; your abuser is already an expert at manipulating you. The most effective form of vengeance is one in which you decide to reclaim your freedom while simultaneously making your abuser irrelevant.

And it will likely crush their ego, and they will feel powerless and helpless in the face of the fact that they cannot even influence you. When it dawns on them that you constantly remind them of their extinction, they are frequently in despair. It is at this point that this comes to an end, and your soul makes a contract with the universe to allow love and healing to enter so that you can once again be whole.

Step 6: Realize Your Liberation, Truth, and Freedom

Traditionally, we learn that loving ourselves is a very selfish act. However, when it comes to finding liberation and freedom from the hands of our abusers, it is a critical step that allows us to take in the truth and let it set us free from captivity. Yes, it is incredibly difficult to do, but it is necessary to achieve liberation. Society has taught us that we are treated by others the same way we treat them. However, this is a false premise because we get treatment according to how we treat ourselves. In other words, the measure of love we get from others is equivalent to what we feel about ourselves.

Strategies To Start Healing From Narcissistic Abuse

While narcissistic abuse can leave behind scars or injuries so deep you may believe you will never be able to completely heal from them, you are still capable of recovering from it. Of course, you can never go back in time. As a result, it is impossible to completely reverse the effects of narcissistic abuse. Still, you can restore yourself to a healthy state of mind through therapy. You can care for yourself and assist yourself in healing. However, even though you may not recognize yourself when you look in the mirror when you are in the grip of abuse, you can reclaim your sense of self. You can reclaim it, and if you are willing to put forth the necessary effort, you will be successful.

Even if your relationship was abusive for an extended period, there is always hope that you will recover. It is possible to heal, and you can do so even though it will be difficult initially. This will guide you through the healing process, step by step, pointing you in the right direction so that you can begin to work on your own health. While working, you will reach a point where you will recognize your own smile in the mirror. You will have peace of mind for the first time in a long time. You will experience renewed happiness and, perhaps, even love. Regardless of what the narcissist has told you, you are capable of change and healing. You deserve to live a life filled with happiness and peace due to your experience. You are deserving of affection. You are deserving of our respect. You deserve to love the person who appears in the mirror when you look in the mirror.

Acknowledge Your Abuse

Healing begins with acknowledgment. You may not be ready for this process if you cannot acknowledge that the narcissist has put you through abuse. By recognizing what happened as the abuse, you will take the steps necessary to correct it and heal. By naming it, you will erase any of the denials you have hidden the abuse behind for however long it occurred. Naming it abuse releases your blame for the abuse. No one asks for their loved ones to hurt them the way the narcissist may have hurt you, nor does anyone deserve it. When you say that the narcissist abused you, you say that the narcissist made a conscious decision to inflict unwanted harm upon you, pushing the blame you may have internalized from yourself onto the narcissist. With that blame lifted, you can begin working on yourself.

As you go through this process, do not forget that you only control yourself. You must be responsible for yourself but do not control how those around you react. Even if you did something as cruel as punching someone on the street, you are not in control of the other person's reaction. You did not deserve what the narcissist did to you, regardless of how minor or extreme the narcissist's manipulation may seem. You were an unfortunate victim, chosen because your traits made you desirable. Instead of lamenting that some of your traits made you a victim, you should celebrate the ones that attract a narcissist—empathy and compassion are fantastic for people. Being patient and seeking peace is an admirable way to live. These are not bad traits to have and do not make you a lesser person. These are traits of a good person. In this situation, the narcissist took advantage of the good person and used your best traits against you. Treat yourself kindly as you consider this, and remember that you did not ask for it to happen.

Forgiveness and Compassion for Yourself

With the acknowledgment of the abuse, you can then move on to forgive yourself. As you established, your traits and strengths should be celebrated, not punished. Forgive yourself for blaming yourself for the abuse so you can begin to celebrate those parts of yourself. You will be able to forgive yourself for not seeing the red flags when they happened, reminding yourself that your good nature may have been to see the good in everyone. Still, ultimately, the narcissist choosing to take advantage of that is not your fault.

You can forgive yourself for not leaving the relationship sooner, reminding yourself that you tried desperately to care for the narcissist, truly loving who they were, and that love was taken advantage of. Your good heart, compassion, and kindness when you see someone suffering were taken advantage of. When you recognize that, you can forgive yourself.

Remember, forgiveness does not necessarily come easy, but you deserve to forgive yourself. You did not intend the situation to get as bad as it did and are trying to heal the best you can. You did your best in the situation with what you had, and that is enough. Yes, you were in a bad situation for some time, but you survived. You were strong enough to cope as it happened, and you were strong enough to say you are ready to get help and begin healing just under having opened this and reading as far as you have. That deserves celebrating as you work through healing.

Remind yourself to give yourself the compassion you would show other people. For example, how would you react if your friend came to you in this situation, telling you your story? Would you be supportive? Would you be kind and understanding? Or would you look at her with a cold, hard look and tell her that she should have tried harder to leave in the beginning? Would you have told her that the abuse was her fault and that she had been asking for it? The answer is most likely no; you would not. Treat yourself with that same compassion as well. You must forgive yourself and treat yourself kindly if you hope to move on toward healing the rest of yourself.

Grieve Properly

Even though your relationship with the narcissist deteriorated and became abusive, you likely still harbored genuine and strong feelings for them. You liked them, or at least the idea they first presented to you when they attempted the love bombing stage when they mirrored your heart's desires, so you fell in love with them. Unfortunately, the idea you fell in love with was quickly annihilated by the narcissist who was left behind, staring back at you with the face of the one you loved as if your loved one had suddenly become possessed by a demon. You have earned the opportunity to mourn the loss of that relationship. However, even though the person you loved was never a real person to you, they were real to you, and as a result, you should allow yourself to grieve their loss. If not for the person you have lost, grieve that you did not receive the relationship you deserved when you fell in love with the narcissist in the first place.

Grief progresses through five stages, which may or may not occur in chronological order. Loss comes and goes, and while you may feel better one day, you may be surprised by feelings of sadness the next when you realize that your relationship with the narcissist has been rekindled. All of this is normal, and grief is one of those things that never completely goes away; you simply learn to live with it.

The denial stage of grief is the first stage of the grieving process. You tell yourself that the relationship does not have to come to an end right away. Your attempt to persuade yourself that what has occurred in your relationship does not warrant a breakup may be fruitless. This is done to protect yourself from the emotional pain you will experience once it is officially over. Second, you go through a period of anger. You have come to terms with the reality in front of you: the narcissist was abusive. At this point, you have come to recognize the narcissist for who they truly are, and this has made you angry. It is enough to send you into a rage just thinking about your abuse or the abuser who inflicted it. Third, you come to the point of bargaining. At this point, the anger has subsided to a certain extent. You convince yourself there are ways or reasons for the relationship to continue working. You tell yourself that the abuse will stop if you just try harder or put in more effort. But it never does. This would be enough to save the relationship, you tell yourself, and you try to grapple with that, even if your bargaining chip ends up being your own wellbeing, such as deciding that you are willing to martyr yourself for the narcissist because you love them. Fourth, you've reached the point of depression. You are acknowledging that the relationship has come to an end. Because you realize that things will never be acceptable, your remaining hope has been shattered. Finally, you come to terms with your situation. At this point, though you may not agree with what happened or that your relationship had to end, you accept the end result and no longer try to fight it.

Release Negative Feelings

As a primary target for a narcissist, you are likely empathetic to some degree. As an empath, you likely tend to absorb the emotions of those around you. You may have internalized some of the narcissist's negativity because of their exposure. You may see some of the narcissist's negative traits in you, such as realizing that you are snapping at people the same way they snapped at you or that you have been thinking about yourself in the way that the narcissist thought of themselves. You might feel uncharacteristically angry at the world. No matter the negative feelings, you need to develop an outlet for them.

If left alone, you may feel as though your very self is festering within you, as though the toxicity from the narcissist still threatens to overwhelm you and turn you into someone you know you are not. The solution to this is to find a good outlet for yourself. Some people pour themselves into a creative hobby, such as drawing, writing, painting, music, dance, or any other form of creating something else. They literally channel their feelings into their art, allowing the negativity to flow through them and into the world so it can no longer consume them. Others choose physical exercise as an outlet, sweating out negativity with each weight set rep or mile run. Others still may decide to nurture something else, such as growing and tending to a garden, bringing back those tender feelings that were once familiar to them. No matter what you choose as your healthy outlet, what is important is that you feel better after engaging in it. You see your general outlook and mood improve the more you do it. Anything is acceptable here, so long as it allows you to channel your negativity in a way that works for you and that you enjoy.

Find Support Networks

Support networks may be one of the most intimidating parts of healing. Support networks imply that you will open up to others about the abuse you endured in person, face to face with others. Some people are not comfortable with this idea. Still, luckily, the internet has made finding groups of people like you easier than ever before.

You can locate both local and online support groups through the internet for the sorts of abuse you endured with your narcissistic partner. You will be able to find someone who has gone through situations eerily similar to your own. You may find that you no longer feel so incredibly, overwhelmingly alone in the world in finding someone else. In addition, you will find people who understand what you have gone through and really mean it when they say they understand.

Your support group will be comprised of others who have survived narcissistic abuse. There will be people on all areas of the healing scale, from still struggling to flee the relationship to having left and thrived after years of work. You will be able to see the progression of life after the narcissist, and knowing that other people have survived and thrived may take away some of the fear and mystery of attempting to heal. You may have had doubts that you would ever feel the same. Still, in finding a group of others who are further along in the process than you are, you will be able to acknowledge that healing is possible. You will see that some people move on to be healthy and productive, and you will be able to strive for that for yourself.

You may even find purpose in helping someone else in a situation like your own in the future, realizing that you will be the one with the ability to aid others and inspire them in their own journeys toward healing.

Self-Care

Taking care of yourself will be extremely important as you heal. You've spent so much time taking care of others, specifically the narcissist, that you deserve to be pampered a little bit yourself. If you truly appreciate who you are, you should go the extra mile for yourself, treat yourself, and remind yourself regularly that you appreciate who you are. Recognizing that you only have one life with one body and appreciate what you have, you should go the extra mile for yourself. Take advantage of this opportunity to spend extra money on bath bombs, if that is your thing, and soak in a long, warm bath to relax and unwind. If you enjoy reading while sipping on a glass of wine, you could even bring one to enjoy while you are soaking wet. You could use the money to pay for a gym membership to get some exercise and improve your stamina. You could decide to enroll in a cooking class and learn how to prepare a few new dishes for yourself now that you have the extra time on your hands. It is acceptable to do anything you have ever wanted to do in this section, as long as it is constructive and aids your overall well-being.

Make certain you nourish your body and mind when taking good care of yourself. You will reap the benefits of caring for yourself like you care for your child. Spend time daily engaging in some form of self-care, whether waking up an hour before work to go for a morning walk or enrolling in a few evening classes to finally learn those new skills you've wanted to learn. Whatever you choose, make sure to set aside plenty of time for self-care. Over time, that level of self-care will become your habitual default, and you will notice that you are far more rested due to your efforts. Taking care of yourself now will allow you to heal from the narcissist's abuse and blossom into the person you would have been had the narcissist not been in your life. You'll start to feel more like yourself again soon after.

Therapy

Trauma, especially from abuse from someone you loved and trusted, can damage a person. You may feel as though you struggle to cope at times or that some of your insecurities that the narcissist has installed are so deeply ingrained that you will never be able to get out from underneath them. Maybe you have no clear idea where to go with your healing and feel like you need guidance. You could benefit from seeking therapy if you are coping with your abuse better or worse than average.

Nearly every single person in this world would benefit from therapy. Therapy teaches us how to better solve problems, cope with negativity, think, and sometimes just help unpack difficult, traumatic events. What you did with the narcissist could be considered traumatic, and you should not hesitate to take advantage of therapy if you think it could be useful to you. With a licensed professional by your side, you will be gently, and without judgment, guided through the healing process with someone prepared to talk you through what is happening. Will addition, you've someone who can pro. This can be absolutely invaluable, especially if your partner was particularly abusive or if you struggle with thoughts of self-harm or suicide or feel your mental health may suffer.

If you feel like getting involved with therapy would be a good option, you should start by asking your primary care physician for a referral, or you can search for therapists in your area on the internet. Do not be deterred because you think therapy is stigmatized. There is nothing wrong with caring for yourself, even if doing so involves getting a professional involved. Remember, no one would think twice if you went to a doctor if you broke your ankle, and struggling with your mental health should be seen no differently. You can do this if you put your mind to it, and you should never let other people make you feel like you are making the wrong choice.

Affirmations

This goes hand-in-hand with self-care but is so important that it deserves its own category. Affirmations are small phrases you repeat to yourself in moments of weakness or when you feel you might make a bad choice that helps you ground yourself in the moment.

Chapter 8: Start Loving Yourself

What is Self-Love, And Why Is It Important To Love Yourself? Why Should You Consider Being Self-Compassionate After?

Over the last fifteen years, there have been numerous studies on happiness, talents, and values. We've all heard that practicing gratitude, for example, can help you overcome a negative self-comparison tendency and increase your appreciation for your possessions. In addition, you may have heard about compassion's social, mental, and physical effects—when you feel moved to help someone in need.
You should also be kind to yourself during major life transitions like divorce. Self-compassion is a Buddhist concept consisting of three parts: seeing your difficulties as part of the universal human struggle, remaining calm and mindful in the face of a traumatic experience rather than allowing it to overwhelm or define you, and seeing yourself with understanding and forgiveness.

What Is Self Care?

Self-care refers to the habits, projects, and practices that enable you to think and feel your best. And for couples, it can be such a loaded term; maybe it makes you cringe because you know you're not doing enough. On the other hand, perhaps the word evokes optimistic emotions because you know you're doing a good job incorporating self-care into your daily routine. You appreciate self-care and want to do more of it! (I mean, who doesn't?) In either case, self-care can be difficult to prioritize, indulgent (as when you get an excellent massage or a deliciously decadent dessert), and difficult to schedule. After all, you are in a long-term relationship with your girlfriend.

In reality, most self-care objections stem from a lack of time, resources, or both. We also associate self-care habits with being time-consuming and/or costly. Even the fact is that

1) you only need 5 minutes at a time for self-care.

2) Self-care does not have to be expensive. It all comes down to the purpose of the operation.

And while the notion that self-care must be indulgent is appealing, there is far more to self-care. There are six major forms of self-care to be aware of, and you should incorporate one of each into your daily routine.

Emotional Self-Care

Emotional self-care entails giving your emotions attention, engaging in behaviors that elicit positive feelings, and coping with negative emotions. This means that coping with the difficult stuff is necessary for self-care.

Mental Self-Care

Taking care of your mental state, doing something mentally stimulating, or working to generate optimistic thinking are examples of mental self-care. Conversely, it can be a formula for disaster if we are not stimulated or mentally engaged.

Physical Self-Care

Physical self-care entails taking care of your body, which includes working out, drinking plenty of water, and keeping important doctor's appointments.

Practical Self-Care

Since it requires daily activities, practicing self-care is often ignored. Cleaning your home, arranging doctor's appointments, and coordinating your family's calendar are examples of self-care.

Social Self-Care

Making time in your life for your friends, relatives, and loved ones is what social self-care is all about. Maintaining connections with others is important for everyone, but particularly for married people. Your "free time" is often consumed by a couple's events and marital obligations. Although you can socialize during those times, spending time with important people is also important.

Spiritual Self-Care

Depending on your values, spiritual self-care can differ. For example, it may imply attending church, praying, or reading religious literature. However, it may also involve activities such as meditation, bonding with nature, or some other practice that feeds the soul. Another important aspect of self-care is taking care of the spirit and mind.

Why Prioritize Self-Care Or Even Be Self-Compassionate?

Even if you don't want to admit it, escaping the trauma of an abusive relationship is difficult. It is not always or every day, but it is difficult. And, because you have a lot on your plate, it's easy to prioritize your partner's needs over your own. But you are entitled to more.

Self-care is essential for happiness and overall well-being, regardless of your situation or circumstances. Self-care allows you to function mentally and physically, and when you're at your best, you can perform better in all aspects of your life. Without it, you risk becoming exhausted, having negative emotions spill over into your interactions with family and friends, and having a mid-life crisis. Conversely, when you're happy and well-cared for, you set the stage for the rest of your life to function properly, including starting to heal.

Practicing To Take Care Of Yourself And Embracing Self Compassion Step by Step

Step 1: Exercising Forgiveness

Stop chastising yourself for your errors. Instead, accept that you are not flawless and be patient with yourself when faced with your flaws. Your friends and colleagues respect you for who you are, not because you are faultless.

Recognize when you get a sense of self-worth from success or excellence. Recognize that you don't have to be a certain way to deserve love.

Place a sticky note near your desk or in your pocket with a message reminding you to be gentle and kind to yourself to remind yourself that you are worthy, even though you aren't doing well.

Punishing the future for mistakes made in the past makes no sense. Instead, let yourself forgive yourself, learn from it, and then let it go.

Step 2: Adopt a Growth Mindset

The effect of our mindset on health is at the core of Carol Dweck's research. She discovered that our satisfaction is influenced by whether we have a fixed or developing mentality. For example, do you see challenges as insurmountable obstacles or chances to grow? A development mentality is more beneficial.

Rather than avoiding obstacles, embrace them, persevere in finding meaning in them, and never give up on yourself. Instead of feeling threatened when you question yourself and harshly compare yourself to others, try to find comfort in their achievements and strengths.

Step 3: Show Your Appreciation

Gratitude is a very strong emotion (Emmons & McCullough, 2003). Rather than longing for something we don't have, there's power in appreciating what we already have right now. You should keep a gratitude journal or go on gratitude walks. By reflecting on our blessings, we use a gentler inner voice and shift the emphasis away from our flaws and toward the world, with all of its beauty.

Step 4: Determine the Appropriate Level of Generosity

Raj Raghunathan (2016) distinguished three types of reciprocity: giver, taker, and matcher. Givers are the most compassionate people, and kindness is an excellent way to express love. But, on the other hand, givers may be the most and least effective individuals, as they can fall into a pattern of selfless giving that ignores their own needs.

Generosity cannot be selfless to benefit your well-being. So, before being generous, ensure you are mindful of your needs. Then, actively select the beneficiary of your generosity, your available resources, and your energy level based on what will benefit your own well-being.

Have fun being charitable as well. See how much of a difference you can make, and don't forget to give back to yourself. Doing something for others makes us happy, but only if it does not hurt our own well-being.

Step 5: Be Conscious

Mindfulness has been shown to positively affect self-compassion by reducing self-judgment (Kabat-Zinn, 2014). Therefore, strive to be present and mindful of what is happening without judgment or marking.

Allow what you think or feel to have its say; don't give it the microphone or bury it in the corner. Instead, allow it to come, and then let it go without attachment.

Self-Care Tips To Follow

What gets in the way of your self-care? Make a list. You'll probably come up with the usual reasons: insufficient time or money, your partner needs you, your schedule is packed, or you don't have the energy. But no matter what your situation, the reality is that *you* are stopping yourself from making self-care happen. You're making excuses, you're prioritizing other people and other things, and you're not intentional with your time. It's okay. We all do it, but you can change. You just need to do a little planning.
Some general things that you can do to take care of yourself may include:

Call a Friend

A text is a quick way to connect with people and get the necessary information. Because of the ease of texting, most of us have gotten away from calling people. In fact, it's easy to be annoyed when the phone rings. But without this old-school form of communication, we miss out on emotional connections with others. It's important to hear the voice of someone you care about and communicate in real-time. Calling may be hard, especially if you have young kids chatting (okay, yelling) in the background, but your friends will understand. You can even text someone first to see if they're available to chat.

Try making your call when your kids are engaged in an activity, or make the call in the car (if you can go hands-free) during your morning commute or after drop-off when your friend might be in the car too, or while you're prepping dinner. Consider starting a regular routine where, every day at the same time, you call your friends to say hi and see how they're doing. Connecting with others is a fundamental need. An adult connection should be a regular part of your day and week. Work to build social and emotional self-care with quick phone calls to friends and family

Practice Mindfulness

Mindfulness is the act of being in the moment, being aware, and taking note of how you think and feel. The idea is to create space between your thoughts, feelings you experience, and how you react without judging yourself— which is a great way to practice mental and emotional self-care.

For this 5-minute activity, sit quietly, observe and experience your surroundings, and focus on your breathing. If thoughts come into your head, label them as you saw in the spilled milk example, then go back to focusing on your breathing. After 5 minutes, you can continue with your day.

You may feel calmer, but the impact will increase as you practice mindfulness. When you repeat this type of self-care consistently, you'll start to notice that you react to situations in a way that's calmer and more controlled, which is better for everyone and your marriage.

Add Flowers to Your Home

Make buying a cheap bouquet on your weekly shopping trip (many stores have $5 bouquets) or cutting flowers from your backyard a habit.

Arrange the flowers in a vase, or several vases if you prefer, and place them where you'll see them frequently but are also out of the way of your children (if you have any). Remember that toddlers can usually reach farther than you think, and older children can always throw balls around the house despite your warnings. Put the flowers on your bedside table to make your room feel more like a personal paradise, or put them in the family room for everyone to enjoy.

This is simple self-care because you're already out shopping. It only takes a few minutes to walk to the flower section and select a bouquet and another few minutes at home to arrange them in a vase.

However, the benefits of emotional self-care will last for days until your next trip to the store to pick up another bouquet. If money is tight, but you like the idea of fresh flowers, request a small bouquet of carnations and baby's breath from the florist, or substitute flowers for one unnecessary grocery item. Allow your partner to bring two bottles of beer; for example, they can have one, and you can have your self-care.

Make a List of Your Friends to Stay in Touch With

It can be difficult to make time to see and speak with others, and even remembering to reach out to some people can be challenging. You can find that you don't see friends who live just a few miles away because their children attend different schools or because you have children of different ages and don't travel in the same circles. Life moves fast, and everyone is busy, so it's easy to lose track of one another.

To counteract this, go through your phone to email, list the people you want to stay in contact with, and schedule get-togethers. Then save this list to your phone or wallet. When you have 5 minutes, go through this list and send texts to say hello or start planning a playdate or an adult date. You have 15 minutes to contact these people to sign in. When you have more time, you should organize meet-ups, playdates, parties, and other activities. This is a practical step to ensuring that you continue to practice social self-care for the people who are important to you. They're worth it, and you are as well.

Watch a Sitcom or Reality-TV

Have trouble deciding how to decompress during your 30 minutes of self-care? Try watching something entertaining on TV!
Sitcoms are an excellent choice because most are only half an hour-long, and many couples enjoy watching reality TV as a guilty pleasure. Drop the guilt and enjoy watching other people's lives in 30-minute increments for this self-care activity. Remember that not all TV shows are created equal for this activity.
Sitcoms and many reality shows are (generally) positive and light in nature, but while you may enjoy dramas and horror shows at other times, choose something that will lead to more positive thoughts and emotions for self-care.
Have you seen a show yet and aren't sure what to watch? Inquire with some of your friends or coworkers about what they're watching. This will allow you to connect in new ways, such as texting about who received the rose on The Bachelor or chatting at work about the latest developments on the show they introduced you to. You can watch a favorite show on Netflix or On Demand, such as Friends, The Office, or How I Met Your Mother.

Engage in Spiritual Practice

Using 30 minutes of your time to devote to your spiritual self-care will feed your soul and likely provide mental and emotional self-care. Of course, it's up to you to determine what spiritual activities meet your needs and how often you want to fit them into your schedule. Still, your spiritual time might be spent listening to a sermon or a religion-based podcast, praying, walking in nature, visiting a place of worship, doing yoga, or engaging in some sort of Bible study or religious group (though you might need more time for some of these activities).

Ideally, your spiritual practice is something you can do without needing childcare (if you have kids). Without much planning, you can fit this in as often as you'd like. Consider making it a regular part of your daily or weekly routine, and find the time that best suits your family's needs and schedule. Maybe you read the Bible or a book that you connect with spiritually aloud as a family. You have a prayer circle together, or you all take time to write in gratitude journals. However, as with all self-care activities, ensure that your spiritual needs are not overshadowed by your family's participation. Young children may struggle with the amount of focus and respect these activities require, and if you are having trouble with your spouse, they might distract you as well. So consider if you want your spiritual practice to be a social affair or not.

It will take time, but these steps will slowly start the healing process. And lastly, I want you to learn how to be grateful again.

Establish Healthy Boundaries

Effective boundaries keep your relationship strong and healthy. Boundaries are limits that you set to protect your well-being. Your partner understands your expectations when boundaries are clearly communicated and the consequences for breaking them. In a previous post, I discussed setting healthy boundaries in your relationship. This post discusses different types of boundaries to consider in your couple's relationship to keep it running smoothly.

To establish effective personal boundaries, you must first understand yourself, communicate your boundaries to others, and then follow through on the consequences. Boundaries exist for and about you. They are about respecting your relationship's needs. For example, resentment can develop when you are unhappy about something in your relationship but do not speak up or share your feelings with your partner. Here are some relationship boundaries to think about to keep your relationship strong.

Physical Boundaries

Your body, privacy, and personal space are all examples of physical boundaries. You may enjoy or be uncomfortable with public displays of affection. If your partner kisses you in public and you are uncomfortable, you must inform them. Sharing your preferences and expectations may be difficult, but failing to do so may make you feel disrespected. It may be simple to draw a line around your partner, not slapping you. In this case, the boundary and consequence may be easy to define. I'll leave if you slap me. However, in some cases, it may be more difficult.

Sharing your personal boundaries can strengthen your bond. Understand what you are and are not comfortable with, and communicate this to your partner. Set a time limit for yourself to decompress after work before socializing with others. This will keep you from feeling exhausted because it will allow you to prioritize your needs. For example, you could say, "I'd like to relax for 15 minutes after work before we invite the neighbors over." Suppose you invite them over before I've relaxed. In that case, I'll go relax in private, leaving you to entertain them until I return.

Emotional Boundaries

You must be in touch with your feelings to establish emotional boundaries. Healthy emotional boundaries necessitate understanding where you end, and your partner begins. For example, a boundary may be necessary if your partner is upset and you notice yourself feeling the same way. Likewise, remember when you feel guilty, ashamed, upset, or undervalued. Again, boundaries may be required if you notice these feelings emerging about specific issues or situations.

If you are upset and your partner tries to help you, you may feel like your partner is not listening to you. Your partner may be trying to help you, but it only makes you feel worse. A boundary could be useful in this situation. You could say that when I'm upset, I want you to listen to me without attempting to fix it. Sometimes I just need to vent. I don't feel heard when you try to fix things. I'll let you know if I need your help.

Sexual Boundaries

Sexual boundaries are your expectations concerning physical intimacy. What is and isn't acceptable to you sexually. Boundaries should be discussed regarding frequency, sexual comments, unwanted sexual touch, expectations regarding others' involvement in your sex life, and what sexual acts are preferred and off-limits. Mutual agreement, mutual consent, and an understanding of each other's sexual limits and desires are all characteristics of healthy sexual boundaries.

A sexual boundary is required if you have been sexually abused in the past and are triggered in certain positions. If you are reminded of a traumatic experience, you should avoid sexual contact with your partner. Setting limits on what is comfortable for you can keep your sex life healthy and happy. For example, you could say that I find it difficult to enjoy a particular sexual position because it reminds me of a difficult experience. Therefore, I need to avoid that position to enjoy sex. I'll let you know if I become irritated so we can switch places.

Intellectual Boundaries

Ideas and beliefs are included within intellectual boundaries. Boundaries around respect for different points of view and ideas can protect your feelings. Talking down to someone or treating them as if they aren't intelligent enough to understand what you're saying can harm your emotional intimacy. A boundary may be necessary if you feel you can't discuss certain topics with your partner because you believe they don't respect your opinion or put you down.

You may feel hurt or upset if you are afraid to express your views or opinions because of your partner's responses. For example, if your partner calls you, A boundary around this can allow you to express yourself honestly. For example, you could say, It bothers me when we disagree politically, and you tell me my point of view is incorrect. It gives me the impression that you don't value my opinions. If you continue to say my opinion is incorrect, I will remind you not to and end the discussion.

Financial Boundaries

It is all about money when it comes to financial boundaries. Boundaries around joint versus separate accounts, how much goes into savings, what purchases you want to make, and how many discretionary funds you will have can help keep you both on the same financial page. Different rules and agendas regarding where and how you spend your money can strain your relationship. If you frequently fight over money, boundaries are probably in order.

Discussions about your financial goals ahead of time can keep money from becoming a source of contention. For example, you may be disappointed if you agree to put money into a separate fund to pay for a vacation and your partner does not contribute. A boundary around this can be beneficial. For example, you might say, "I want to go on a nice vacation with you," but for that to happen, we both need to contribute to the vacation fund. I'll match if you tell me when and how much you're putting into the fund.

Boundaries allow your relationship to function properly. When you notice that you are being disrespected, taken advantage of, or hurt, you should think about how setting a boundary can help. Knowing and respecting your personal limits and needs can help improve and sustain your couple's relationship.

How Meditation And Positive Affirmation Can Help To You

Narcissistic abuse is a form of emotional and psychological abuse that happens when one person in a relationship controls and exploits another for their own benefit. It can be incredibly damaging to the victim, leaving them feeling humiliated, alone, and scared.

However, with the help of meditation and positive affirmation, you can begin to heal from narcissistic abuse - regardless of its severity. In this article, we'll discuss the benefits of meditation and how you can use it to address narcissistic abuse in your life.

How Positive Affirmations Can Help?

Positive affirmation can be a powerful tool to help heal from narcissistic abuse. It can help you reassert yourself and your identity, counterbalance the negative thoughts and feelings that may result from narcissistic abuse and develop self-compassion.

To use positive affirmation effectively, ensure it aligns with your personal values and beliefs. Second, be mindful of how you are using it. Third, be patient with yourself – you may take longer than others to recover from narcissistic abuse, and positive affirmation should not be the only thing helping you heal. Finally, remember that the process of healing is ongoing – keep working towards your goals, and don't be discouraged if progress is slow at first.

How Meditation Can Help?

People who have been through narcissistic abuse may find relief and healing in meditation. For example, in a study published in the journal "Personality and Social Psychology Review," meditation was an effective tool for reducing rumination, a common symptom of narcissistic abuse.
Ruminative thinking is a pattern of thought that revolves around negative self-judgment and obsessive thoughts about the past. It can lead to feelings of sadness, guilt, and worthlessness. People who suffer from narcissistic abuse often engage in ruminative thinking because it helps them deal with their fear of abandonment.
Meditation is an effective way to reduce rumination in people who don't usually engage in negative thinking. In fact, one study found that people who meditated showed a decrease in rumination compared to people who didn't meditate. This suggests that meditation can help people break the cycle of narcissistic abuse.
The benefits of meditation don't stop there. Meditation has also been found to reduce anxiety and stress levels. Considering how common it is for people who have experienced narcissistic abuse to experience high levels of anxiety and stress, this is definitely something to consider if you're looking for relief from narcissistic abuse.
Meditation can be a powerful tool for healing from narcissistic abuse. If you or someone you know is struggling with narcissistic abuse, consider trying meditation as an effective way to reduce rumination and anxiety.
If you have been the victim of narcissistic abuse, then you know how it feels to be constantly criticized and put down. It's hard to feel good about yourself when you're being treated this way, which is why escaping narcissism can be daunting. However, there are ways out, and healing can happen if you take the time to find them. By learning about meditation and positive affirmation, you can start to rebuild your self-esteem and work towards a healthier relationship with yourself moving forward.

The Basics Of Mediation: What Exactly Is Meditation?

Meditation is a simple way to relax the mind. It is one of the most basic methods for temporarily removing yourself from the inner chaos of your mind and gaining a rational understanding of what is happening. In addition, it is the most effective way to untangle complex ideas.
Above all, it is a way to bring harmony and peace into your life.
We all have problems in this race called life. In our heads, a hundred different things are going on. According to the most conservative estimates, the human mind has approximately 50000 thoughts per day. Even if only a small percentage of these thoughts are negative, upsetting, or problematic, they can hurt one's life. Unfortunately, most of us have a high proportion of such negative emotions. As a result of these reflections, the mind is constantly devising strategies and counterstrategies. It is not something that can be actively influenced. It can be difficult to quiet your mind, even for a short period. Such thoughts will keep you awake at night. The more you try to ignore these feelings, the more violent they become.
Meditation is a technique for temporarily quieting the mind. It's a simple exercise that will help you gain control of your thoughts and emotions. You'd be able to clear your mind before refilling it with positive thoughts. Meditation time allows you to pick and choose which ideas to critically examine. You can isolate each negative thought in your mind and choose to discard it permanently. Meditation will give you tremendous control over your thought process and, as a result, your life.
It can effectively treat your sorrows, worries, anxieties, hatred, and general life confusion. It is one of the most powerful ways to completely change one's mind. You could achieve thoughtless consciousness. This will clear your mind and relax and center you within.

Meditation can help you figure out what's causing your mental problems. It is a profound mental state in which you can see and make better decisions. The best thing about meditation is that no special equipment is required. All you have to do is sit, stand, or walk quietly. You can perform the procedure whenever you want once you're comfortable with it. You will have complete control over your life and will be able to find the happiness you seek. As a result, you'll be happier, more fulfilled, and more at ease.

Modern life has devolved into a race in which we all compete for no discernible goal. There is no winner in this race because there is no finish line. Meditation will provide you with the clarity you require to enjoy the race.

How Does Meditation Work?

A person in a meditative state may appear to be an idle person sitting in a cross-legged posture with eyes closed to a bystander. There is no complication. To meditate, one does not even need to be in this position. You can meditate while sitting, walking, or even lying on the ground.

While in a meditative state, the body appears inactive, but the mind is very active. In the meditative state, you can unravel some of the most complex mysteries of the mind.

On a physical level, meditation has a significant impact on brain activity. It aids in the clearing of the mind as well as the attainment of objective focus. Every significant thought that enters your mind results in a specific type of chemical reaction. Positive thinking has a calming effect. Happy thoughts cause the release of chemicals that reduce anger and anxiety. Conversely, when you have many negative, stressful, and fearful thoughts, your body produces more stress hormones. Not only will this cause emotional distress, but it will also weaken your immune system.

A person attempting to lose weight will find it extremely difficult to burn fat while stressed or emotional. The reason for this is an increase in stress hormone production. This hormone keeps the body in a constant state of fat storage. Meditation is an excellent way to relax the mind and the nervous system. It increases activity in specific brain regions and reduces anxiety and depression. In addition, your body develops a higher pain tolerance. Finally, meditation helps to improve memory, self-awareness, and goal-setting abilities.

When our brain is active, it generates fast and choppy beta waves. In this state, thoughts can become jumbled. There are too many thoughts going through my head simultaneously, and I have very little control over them. However, while meditating, the brain begins to produce slow alpha waves. These waves are calming. The stress level begins to decrease. The rambling of thoughts also decreases. You will begin to feel more in control of your mind in this state. These waves are linked to feelings of love, optimism, and happiness. As one practices meditation for a longer period, the level of alpha waves increases.

Meditation can cause physical changes in your brain's shape and size. Meditation has been shown in studies on long-term practitioners to increase grey matter in specific brain areas.

There are two critical areas to consider:

Insular Cortex: This area is associated with breathing and heartbeat awareness. The longer you meditate, the better your breathing and heart will be. This would imply that your body would be better able to transport oxygen and carbon dioxide. As a result, you would be more resistant to diseases.

Premotor Cortex: This area is in charge of controlling attention, emotions, and thoughts. If the grey matter in this area becomes denser, your learning and memory abilities will improve. You would be more in control of your emotions and thoughts.

The Amygdala is the part of your brain that deals with stress, fear, and anxiety. Meditation has clearly been shown in studies to help reduce grey matter in this area. It can significantly aid in the reduction of stress, fear, high blood pressure, and immune-related disorders.

With enough practice, your brain can begin to produce gamma waves. These waves can aid in the development of intense concentration and unwavering focus. Aside from the physiological benefits, meditation can help you improve your ability to manage your thoughts and emotions.

Our minds are frequently perplexed by the distinction between wants and needs. The issues arise when it begins to use the terms interchangeably. We have high expectations of people, jobs, relationships, personal wealth, and other things. When they are not met, we begin to have negative thoughts. Meditation allows you to see your thoughts objectively. You can judge the futility of desires and understand the true value of things. This can make life a lot easier. The most important things in life are not even required, but we waste our lives pursuing them. We simply follow them indefinitely because we see others doing the same. We develop a herd mentality and become engrossed in the mind-numbing rat race. Meditation lets you objectively analyze your thoughts, needs, and desires to determine the best course of action. Meditation sessions make you feel much more calm, relaxed, and peaceful. Decisions would become easier, and your mind would not constantly be battling decision fatigue. Your ability to look at things objectively would improve, as would your perspective.

Why Does Meditation Work?
With mindfulness meditation increasing in popularity, there has been an explosion of studies to understand its effects. As reported in Neuroreport and Psychiatry Research, researchers found that after eight weeks of mindfulness practice, there were significant effects on the brain.

Four parts of the brain linked to healthy brain function saw significant positive changes: the left hippocampus, which is associated with learning and houses emotional regulators, such as self-awareness and empathy; the posterior cingulate, which is connected with wandering thoughts and self-relevance; the pons, where neurotransmitters that help regulate brain activity are produced; and the temporoparietal junction, which is associated with compassion and our sense of perspective. These parts grew in size, volume, density, or strength, resulting in all the qualities of these regions being nurtured.

Furthermore, the amygdala, the brain area that produces feelings of anxiety, stress, and fear, decreased in size. This change allows us to discern our emotional responses more clearly.

Why Should You Practice Meditation?

Most things you might have tried to date take some time to show results. Meditation is a unique practice that starts showing results instantaneously. The day you begin meditation, you will start experiencing a positive change in your stress and anxiety levels. You will feel more relaxed and calm. A feeling of joy emerges from inside when you start practicing meditation. Besides these, meditation has many more benefits that you will experience as you start practicing it longer.

1. **Makes You Happier:** Meditation has a great calming effect on the mind. You start feeling relaxed and joyful. There is a feeling of inner bliss. The brain's flow of constructive thoughts increases, making meditators feel joyful.
2. **Reduces Anxiety, Stress, And Depression:** Our brain has a specific amygdala regulating stress, anxiety, and depression. Studies have shown that meditation can lead to a reduction in the size of these areas. Therefore, if you practice meditation regularly, you will significantly reduce your stress and anxiety levels.
3. **Instant Results:** The positive impact of meditation can be noticed from the very first session. You will start feeling relaxed

and calm from the very beginning. You wouldn't have to wait for months to notice the positive effect.

4. **Improves Sleep:** Meditation has a very strong impact on your sleep patterns. The people who meditate find significant improvement in their sleep. They can sleep better and wake up more relaxed and calm. Sleep deprivation is a problem that affects many people these days. It not only increases stress levels but also severely impacts overall health. Meditation can help a lot in this area. It helps you fall asleep much faster.

5. **Sharpens Memory:** Meditation improves memory. This is because your mind gets trained to live in the present and analyze thoughts objectively. This also means that it learns the ways to retain important things strongly. As a result, your memory sharpens over a while as you meditate.

6. **Brings Clarity:** One of the most significant advantages of meditation is that it helps you achieve a state of thoughtless awareness. This is the state where you can look at everything in your mind in a non-judgmental way. As a result, your perspective improves, and you can get better clarity of thoughts. The reactionary thought process stops, and you can look at things objectively.

Brief Meditation Techniques For A Stress-Free Life

Numerous studies, including one at Harvard University, have shown that meditation has numerous physiological benefits. For example, during the eight-week study, researchers discovered that a simple practice like meditation could rebuild the brain's grey matter in as little as eight weeks.

The brain's grey matter is in charge of the brain's primary thinking, perceiving, and cognitive functions, which aid in information processing. So meditation can help you with much more than just boosting your brain; it can also help you lower your blood pressure, fight anxiety, cope with pain, and deal with stress.

Here are a few quick meditation techniques you can use no matter where you are!

The 4-7-8 Technique

The 4-7-8 breathing exercise is also a simple technique. It entails breathing in a while, counting to four, holding the breath for seven counts, and exhaling for eight counts.

This technique is a natural nervous system relaxant. However, you should not take more than four breaths at first because it may cause dizziness.

1. Sit with your back straight and your shoulders relaxed.
2. Place the tip of your tongue against the tissue behind your upper front teeth and keep your tongue in place while breathing.
3. Inhale four times through your nose.
4. Take a deep breath and hold it for seven seconds.
5. Exhale for about eight seconds through your mouth.
6. This is considered one breath cycle. You can do this three or four times more.

The 4-7-8 ratio is the most important aspect of this exercise. If you find it difficult to hold your breath for seven seconds, you can speed up the practice. Once you've mastered this technique, you'll be able to use it to combat stress whenever it arises.

Breath Counting Method

Another beneficial exercise is counting your breaths.
- Sit with your back straight and in a comfortable position. Close your eyes and naturally take a few deep breaths in and out.
- As you inhale, mentally count to one and exhale slowly.
- Inhale again, count to two, and exhale slowly.
- Repeat this cycle as long as you want, counting as you go.

Aim for a ten-minute breathing session.

Body Scan Meditation

1. Body scan meditation, also known as body awareness, is an exercise that allows you to tune out distractions while focusing on different parts of your body. Body scanning is an excellent technique for becoming more aware of how you feel at any given time. For example, excessive muscle tension aggravates muscle pain, headaches, and fatigue, and scanning the body can help you avoid pressure buildup. You have the option of performing a quick body scan or a more thorough scan. A quick scan can help you release tension quickly, and it only takes a few seconds.
2. Put yourself in a comfortable position. You have the option of sitting or lying down.
3. Close your eyes for more in-depth practice.
4. Tune into and pay attention to any sensations you feel, such as pain or discomfort, beginning with your feet and toes. You may also experience tingling, stinging, aching, or throbbing sensations.
5. Take a deep breath in through your nose and exhale through your mouth to relieve the discomfort. Then, allow your body to release, loosen, and soften.
6. Work your way up the body, focusing on the legs, hips, back, stomach, chest, neck and shoulders, arms and hands, and finally, the face, paying attention to how you feel as you go.
7. Gradually work your way up to your body, focusing on each muscle group one at a time.

The Technique Of Visualization

Visualization is a lovely way to calm and relax the body, which can also aid in sleep (Raypoole, 2020). You are daydreaming and visualizing whenever you use your imagination. Visualization for relaxation and sleep employs the imagination to create a mental location in which the mind and body can be calm and relaxed.

Visualization aids in the relaxation of the mind and body by clearing away the day's clutter. You can practice seeing things with all of your senses while visualizing. Visualization, also known as Guided Imagery, is an excellent way to take a mental vacation.

1. Begin by closing your eyes and picturing a peaceful and relaxing place in your mind, such as a beach or a park.
2. Allow your imagination to use all of your senses to feel and see everything. For example, feel the sun's warmth, listen to the waves, or observe the birds.
3. If you have stressful thoughts, acknowledge them and then dismiss them.

Gratitude Meditation

It is extremely powerful to pause for a moment and practice gratitude. A 2015 study found that mindfulness-based gratitude practices were associated with increased happiness and decreased stress (O'Leary & Dockray, 2015).

- Close your eyes and think about something small you are noticing. This could be as simple as seeing a tree outside or feeling warm.
- Next, consider someone who has had an influence on your life. This could be someone you know or someone you don't know.

- Express your gratitude for everything you're thankful for, such as a hot cup of coffee in the morning or a good friend.
- And don't forget to be grateful for your healthy body and the presence of mind that allows you to be here in this moment.
- Allow yourself as much time as you need to meditate and reflect.

Walking Meditation

Walking meditation is the simplest form of meditation. Walking meditation is a great option for those who enjoy being outside or have difficulty sitting still and clearing their minds. Walking meditation entails walking silently and contemplatively. Walking benefits the mind, body, and spirit (Hanh, 2011). For example, if you are stressed, one of the best things you can do is get outside, move around, and take a break. It is simple to go for a short or long walk, and it can help relieve stress and anxiety.
Walking meditation is an excellent option for those who have difficulty sitting still. Incorporating a simple walking meditation into your day is a wonderful way to relieve stress. Walking meditation aims to become more aware of what is happening in the present moment (Hanh, 2011). Walking meditation can be done anywhere, but a park or other area with greenery or foliage is ideal.
This Walking Meditation is based on the guided walking meditation developed by mindfulness expert Jon Kabat-Zinn.

- Begin by locating a suitable location, preferably quiet and not likely to be disturbed or observed.
- Take 10-15 steps, then pause and breathe for as long as you want.
- Take note of your surroundings. Take a moment to reflect on the trees, foliage, flowers, and even the ground you're standing on. Take note of all the minor details.
- You can also observe while walking. The goal of the practice is to walk silently and with deep contemplation.
- You can also concentrate on the sound of your footsteps as you walk and how your feet strike the ground.
- A walking meditation entails deliberate thinking and performing a series of actions that you would normally perform automatically.
- As you walk, try to concentrate on one or more sensations that you normally take for granted, such as

your breathing, the movement of your legs, or how the air feels against your skin.

If your mind wanders, return your attention to something specific in your surroundings.

Positive Affirmations To Say Every Day

- I allow unconditional love to follow me wherever I go.
- I open myself to the love and beauty of life, and I accept it now.
- I move beyond forgiveness to understanding and have compassion and kindness for others and myself.
- I accept that I am an unlimited being and that I can create anything I want.
- I treat myself with gentle, loving kindness at all times.
- I am worthy of my own love and affection.
- Today is a great day to start truly loving myself.
- I end each day with a shower of love and appreciation for myself.
- I love the person I am and the one I am becoming.
- I am a unique gift to this world, and I rejoice in sharing this gift every day. Little by little, I am accepting myself more each day.
- I accept myself how I am; I am free to be me.
- I have compassion for myself.
- I look at people with love in my heart.
- I love all of life.
- I love praising others and accept praise with ease.
- I am worthy of sincere, affectionate love.
- I am a well-loved and respected person.
- I give myself a chance to be loved.
- My parents express their love for me in the best way they know. Likewise, my siblings and I support and love each other.
- I am one with the power of love.
- I deserve a happy family life, and I accept it now.

Conclusion

I would like to convey my heartiest gratitude for reading this book through to the end. I sincerely hope you found the information in this draft helpful and insightful.

Escaping from a narcissistic relationship isn't an easy thing to do. In fact, you have quite the task ahead of you. The task involves taking back your life before it's too late.

There will be times when you wish to return. You feel a strong tug from that trauma bond, and all you want to do is run back to what you now consider "safety" with the narcissist. You feel the discomfort of cognitive dissonance within yourself and want to alleviate it by any means possible.

When this occurs, keep in mind that you are far from finished processing your emotions concerning the abusive experience. You still have some issues to work through. So don't be too hard on yourself. It's fine. Remember, this isn't going away overnight; rather than being discouraged by your desire to return, allow those feelings to motivate you to continue your work of self-healing.

Remember to stay in the moment while also planning for the future. This is the only way to truly save yourself while creating a better version of yourself. Now is the time to think about your dreams and see how you can bring them to life or dream even bigger!

When you have a strong sense of purpose and passion, you will find that you barely have time to reflect on your past. Instead, you believe in welcoming the future with open arms. This allows you to let go of the narcissistic injury you've experienced, propelling you forward and upwards to heights you'd never imagined.

You will need to learn to listen to yourself as you progress through this healing process. A quiet, firm voice within us desires the best for us. It is constantly speaking. We'd hear it if we just paid attention. Check in with yourself regularly and ask yourself how you are feeling. When you're about to make a decision, check in with that voice and listen to how you feel about your options. You'll discover that you can rely on the answers you receive from within.

Finally, be gentle with yourself. Don't be upset because you make mistakes from time to time. You're only human, after all. We, humans, are prone to making mistakes. That is not to say you haven't made any progress. If anything, be relieved when you realize you've made a mistake again because it allows you to see where and how you can improve and grow. Everyone learns, grows, and heals at a different pace. So be gentle with yourself. Be gentle and loving. Show yourself the love you deserve, and you'll be completely free and healed before you know it.

You can do it if you take it one step at a time.

CPSIA information can be obtained
at www.ICGtesting.com
Printed in the USA
BVHW091322290922
648302BV00016B/706